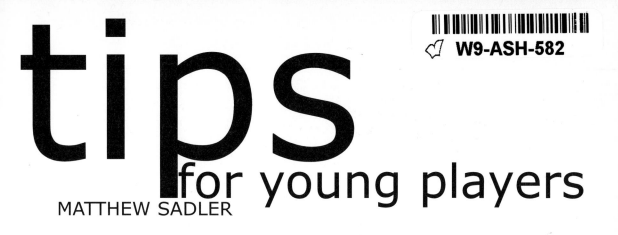

tips
for young players

MATTHEW SADLER

EVERYMAN CHESS

First published 1999 by Everyman Publishers plc, formerly Cadogan Books plc, Gloucester Mansions, 140A Shaftesbury Avenue, London WC2H 8HD

British Library Cataloguing-in-Publication Data
A catalogue record for this book is available from the British Library.

ISBN 1 85744 231 8

Distributed in North America by The Globe Pequot Press, 6 Business Park Road, P.O. Box 833, Old Saybrook, Connecticut 06475-0833.
Telephone 1-800-243 0495 (toll free)

All other sales enquiries should be directed to Everyman Chess, Gloucester Mansions, 140A Shaftesbury Avenue, London WC2H 8HD
tel: 0171 539 7600 fax: 0171 379 4060
email: dan@everyman.uk.com
website: www.everyman.uk.com

To Maaike

EVERYMAN CHESS SERIES (formerly Cadogan Chess)
Chief Advisor: Garry Kasparov
Advisory Panel: Andrew Kinsman and Byron Jacobs

Typeset and edited by First Rank Publishing, Brighton
Production by Book Production Services
Printed and bound in Great Britain by The Cromwell Press Ltd., Trowbridge, Wiltshire

Contents

Chapter One

The Opening:
General Principles

- ■ **Control of the Centre**
- ■ **King Safety**
- ■ **Rapid Development**
- ■ **The Initiative**

Everyone who tries to learn more about chess feels from time to time as if they have been thrown in at the deep end with no idea how to swim or where to go! There are whole books about single openings which contain reams and reams of analysis. You can try to memorise this material, but too often the question arises 'Why on earth did White (or Black) do that?' with no explanation in sight!

In the race to explain what is happening on, say, move 14, strong players often forget that at some stage they had to set out from the same point as any beginner: starting from scratch, building from nothing. How did these players make progress, and how did this shape the openings and variations that top players play today?

Although the analysis of the leading players is often extremely deep, their choices are still based on four general principles of the opening. Before we get down to any of the practical skills of building an opening repertoire, we really need to understand each of the following simple concepts in turn:

1. Control or occupation of the centre
2. King safety
3. Rapid development
4. The initiative

Control or Occupation of the Centre

Why exactly is the centre of the board so vital in chess?

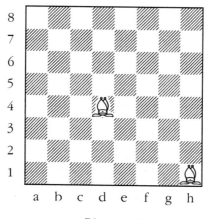

Diagram 1
The dark-squared bishop is stronger

The answer is simple mathematics (see diagram 1):

Q. How many squares does the d4-bishop attack?
A. Thirteen (we don't include the square that it stands on)

Q. How many squares does the h1-bishop control?
A. Only seven, a lot less than the dark-squared bishop!

Right, so let's try the same thing with the knights!

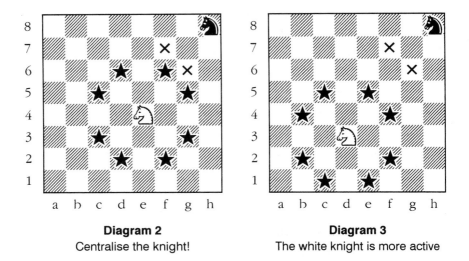

Diagram 2
Centralise the knight!

Diagram 3
The white knight is more active

Q. How many squares does the white knight control in diagram 2?
A. A powerful eight.

Q. How many squares does the black knight control?
A. Merely two.

The trend is clear! *Pieces attack more squares from the centre of the board than from the side of the board.* The more squares a piece attacks, the more influence it has on the board, and the greater its mobility. For example, in diagram 3 White's knight can move to the kingside or the queenside, or advance further in the centre. All that Black's knight can do is to hobble around on the kingside.

TIP: Pieces have more activity nearer the centre. Having active pieces will give you the intiative.

But why should you want to occupy the centre with pawns? Well, take a look at this example (see diagram 4):

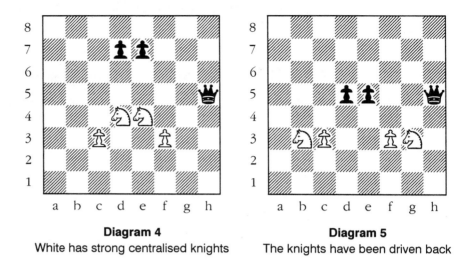

Diagram 4
White has strong centralised knights

Diagram 5
The knights have been driven back

White's knights are powerfully placed in the centre aren't they? Surely Black's queen, the most powerful piece on the board, can shift them? Um, well no actually! Black can attack both knights with 1...Qd5, but there is no threat. Both knights are protected by pawns. If Black takes either of the knights, White will win a queen for a knight. So what can two little pawns do where a queen has failed? Quite a lot actually, as we shall see:

1...e5! Black attacks the knight on d4. It has to move, or it will be captured. It is not a good deal for White to lose a knight for a pawn. **2 Nb3 d5!** Now Black attacks the other knight. It also has to move, or it will be taken. **3 Ng3** (see diagram 5).

Look at the position. The knights have now been driven from their powerful central posts! This was only possible because of the relatively low ranking of the pawns. Because they are the least valuable unit on the board, pawns are extremely useful in preventing your opponent from taking control of the centre with pieces! When the queen attacked the knights, by contrast, it offered no threat at all.

This gives us a general rule: *pawns clear the way for the pieces.* Think of pawns as hard-working bulldozers, pushing aside obstacles so that the fast cars – the pieces – have a clear road ahead. Eventually, you want to place your pieces in the centre. However, first you must occupy the centre with your pawns in order to stop the opponent from establishing a foothold there.

TIP: Use your pawns as a mechanism to clear the way for your pieces.

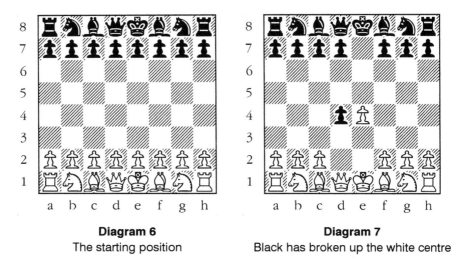

Diagram 6
The starting position

Diagram 7
Black has broken up the white centre

Imagine that you are White and your opponent says to you, 'I give you two free moves at the start!' What would you play?

That's right, 1 d4 and 2 e4 (or 1 e4 and 2 d4), occupying the centre with pawns. There is a snag though: this never happens; the opponent always has a move as well! This is always the problem in chess – *it is never possible to achieve all your aims right from the start.* For example, after **1 e4** Black often plays **1...e5**. If you then go **2 d4** Black can play **2...exd4** (see diagram 7) and... you don't have two pawns in the centre! You didn't do anything wrong on the first move. It's just the nature of chess that you can't get everything you want. *The whole game of chess, and the opening in particular, is like bartering with your opponent.* You say 'I want this.' He says 'No.' So you say, 'I want this, but I will give you this other little thing if you give it to me.' Your opponent thinks 'Well, I want that... Okay, I'll give him what he wants.' The better chessplayer is the one who judges best what it is important and what can be disregarded.

 TIP: In the opening try to establish a strong pawn front in the centre.

King Safety

The ultimate aim in every game of chess is to checkmate the opponent's king. This is done either by a direct attack, or by winning so many of the opponent's pieces that the king is completely defenceless. The king is the most precious and the most vulnerable piece on the board – it is the one piece that you cannot afford to lose. And what do you do with something valuable? You hide it in a safe place; somewhere people would not normally go. And so it is with the king.

The king starts the game in the centre. At the beginning of the game, this is not a problem because the opponent's pieces are undeveloped and so cannot create threats. But soon enough the king will become exposed if it stays where it is. Why is this? Well, in order to develop your pieces, you have to start moving pawns. For example, in order to develop his king's bishop on f1, White's simplest option is to play **1 e4** (see diagram 9).

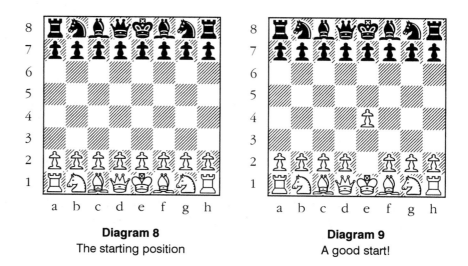

Diagram 8
The starting position

Diagram 9
A good start!

This opens the diagonal from f1 to a6. It is a good move, but note that there is no longer a pawn directly shielding the white king. Whenever a pawn moves forward to gain space, away from its 'friends', it inevitably becomes less easy to protect. As this pawn is now slightly more vulnerable, the king automatically becomes a little more insecure on e1.

The basic opening aim of both sides is to impose their will in the centre. In such a struggle, the centre often becomes opened.

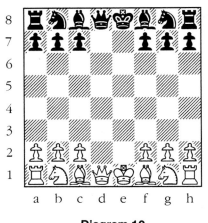

Diagram 10
The centre is opened up

What function does the king perform on the e-file in the type of position shown in diagram 10? The queens on d1 and d8 attack seven squares each on the d-file. However, the kings attack only one square each on the e-file, and pose no threat to any of the opponent's pieces. Now if one side had a rook on the e-file, the opponent would be in severe difficulties... So where should the king go in the opening?

To one of the wings. In the opening, the fight will normally be in the centre. The wing pawns – g- and h-; a- and b- – will be left untouched as there is no reason to push them. *The king is always safest behind pawns left on the second rank (they are as far from the opponent's pieces as possible) and away from open files.*

 TIP: Keep a look out for tactical opportunities if your opponent has kept his king in the centre too long – you may be able to deliver a quick knockout.

It is always very important to castle, either kingside (the most normal) or queenside early on if possible. In order to achieve this, there is something we need...

Rapid Development

Speed and efficiency are as important in chess as in every aspect of life. If you want to win a race, it helps to be faster than your opponents! The quicker you activate your pieces, the faster you can get your king to safety. The more quickly you develop, the sooner you can attack the opponent's position. Obviously, there is a limit to how fast you can develop: you only have one move at a time! *But you should always try to play your pieces to good central posts in one move. Never spend two or three moves on one piece at the expense of the rest of your pieces unless you are forced to do so.* The reason for this is simple. Both sides have the same number of pieces to start with. You cannot overcome a well-matched opponent with just a couple of pieces – you need all of them in the action. The Ruy Lopez, one of the oldest openings, provides an illustration:

1 e4 e5 2 Nf3 Nc6 3 Bb5 a6 4 Ba4 The bishop was attacked, so it had to move. **4...Nf6 5 0-0 Be7 6 Re1** (see diagram 11)

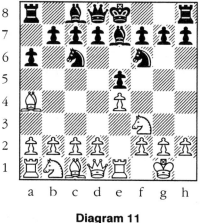

Diagram 11
Solid play from both sides

White has castled extremely quickly. *Note that castling is an excellent developing move as it brings the rook on h1 closer to the crucial central files.*

With his king tucked away on the kingside, White is now ready to start playing in the centre. His bishop already has some influence here as it attacks the knight on c6, which is defending Black's central pawn on e5 from capture by the white knight.

We can see how all these factors are connected. You want to fight for control of the centre because your pieces are at their most powerful there. Because the fight in the opening revolves around the centre, you want to spirit your king away from the centre as quickly as possible. You also need your king where the 'scenery' is undisturbed: on the wings, either the kingside or the queenside. Finally, you need to get your pieces out as quickly and as efficiently as possible so that you can achieve all this and begin active operations.

 WARNING: Unless forced, don't move the same piece twice in the opening. Early in the game time is crucial – don't waste it.

The Initiative

The annoying thing about chess is that you can't follow general rules blindly and expect to be successful. Why not? Are these general rules useless? Not at all! They are the most important things that you will ever learn in chess. But to take a simple analogy, the aim of both sides in a football match is to score a goal. But only one side can score at one time – the side that has the ball! However much the other side wants to score, they can't do anything until they win the ball back. In chess terms, you would say that the side with the ball has the initiative – *it has the power to make things happen.*

This factor is the one that places obstacles in the path of general principles. It doesn't invalidate them, but it makes them harder to implement. We can best understand this by looking again at the Ruy Lopez.

1 e4 e5 2 Nf3 Nc6 3 Bb5 a6 (see diagram 12)   *if Nxe5 Qd4*

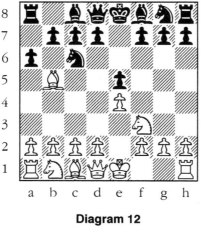

Diagram 12
The Ruy Lopez

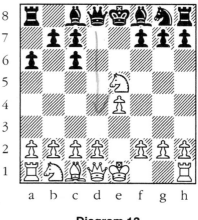

Diagram 13
Can White win a pawn?

Q. I wanted to ask you. Can't White just win a pawn now by 4 Bxc6 dxc6 5 Nxe5? (see diagram 13)

A. No, because 5...Qd4! forks the knight on e5 and the pawn on e4. Now 6 Nf3 Qxe4+ wins the pawn back with a good position.

So this 'threat' does not quite work yet, but you could imagine circumstances where it might work for White, once he has developed more pieces.

4 Ba4 Nf6 5 0-0 Be7 6 Re1 (see diagram 14)

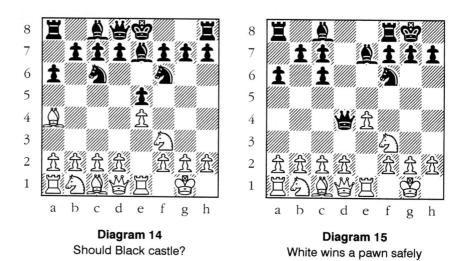

Diagram 14
Should Black castle?

Diagram 15
White wins a pawn safely

Q. So what is the most logical move in this position?

A. 6...0-0 getting the king to safety. However, this is a blunder since now White *can* win a pawn with 7 Bxc6 dxc6 8 Nxe5 as the pawn on e4 is now protected by the rook on e1. After 8...Qd4 9 Nf3! (see diagram 15) Black is no longer able to capture on e4.

White holds the power to make things happen at the moment. Here he is using it to interfere with Black's attempts to carry out the general opening principles. But just because there is a little interference, it doesn't mean that the general principles have to be abandoned altogether. A normal continuation here is **6...b5**, cutting out the attack of the bishop on a4 on the knight on c6. This makes the pawn on e5 safe. **7 Bb3** and now **7...0-0** (see diagram 16)

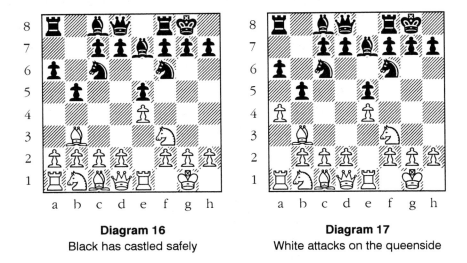

Diagram 16
Black has castled safely

Diagram 17
White attacks on the queenside

The principles have been achieved, but White's initiative at least forced Black to play one specific move (6...b5) before he could get his king to safety.

This is a typical moment in the opening. Note how with 3 Bb5, White developed actively by putting pressure on Black's position – you can't make somebody fall without touching them!

Q. A couple more queries. What did White achieve finally through 3 Bb5? After move 7, hasn't Black got everything he wants?

A. When the opponent plays good moves from the start, developing sensibly whilst dealing with specific threats, you cannot hope to get a dramatic advantage from the opening. You should compare your task to unravelling a garment by pulling on a loose thread – one thread leads to another loose thread until everything finally falls apart. Remember what I said about pawns advancing: *the closer pawns come to the opponent's forces, the more vulnerable to attack they become.* White can claim that 6...b5 is the first weakness – the first loose thread – and that by attacking this pawn he can force another concession, and then another, etc. For example, from the diagram, **8 a4** (see diagram 17) is a common continuation, attacking the pawn on b5. White threatens 9 axb5 winning a pawn, because 9...axb5 is impossible due to 10 Rxa8 picking up a rook.

By forcing the pawn forward to b5, White has created a little target, a fresh way for him to 'tickle' Black's position. This is not a disaster for Black, but White is simply the one making things happen at the start. Why is this? What did Black do wrong? Absolutely nothing. Just remember that White moves first! Inevitably, he can castle earlier than Black; he can put pressure on Black's position first. Therefore, it is not surprising that he can claim the initiative first. Having the white pieces is often compared to having the serve at tennis – you get to choose the early direction of the struggle, the general pattern of the game. Black's first task in the opening is always to counter White's initiative and to get his own position in order. But Black nearly always finds that he has to make maybe a couple of moves he wouldn't normally play (6...b5 for example) in order to achieve this.

However, the most important thing to remember is that neither side can possibly get everything they want from the opening if the opponent plays reasonably. So you have to be sensible! Remember also that as White has the first move, he always has a little more time than his opponent; consequently if anyone can get away with strange moves in the opening, it is more likely to be him than Black!

Try it Yourself

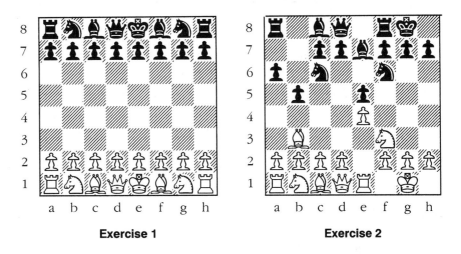

Exercise 1

Exercise 2

Exercise 1 You are White. Imagine that you can make five consecutive moves! With them, I want you to: a) Occupy the centre; b) Develop two pieces; c) Put your king to safety.

Exercise 2 What you think about the following two moves: a) 8 h4? and b) 8 a4?

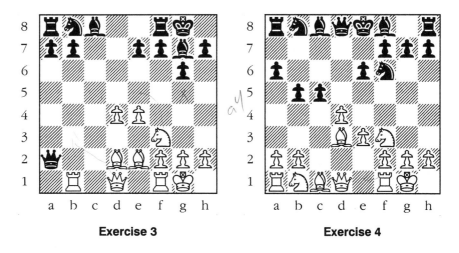

Exercise 3

Exercise 4

Exercise 3 Find the 'grandmaster move' that puts pressure on Black's position.

Exercise 4 This is a position from the Queen's Gambit Accepted. Find a way to put pressure on Black's position.

Summary

Pieces attack more squares from the centre of the board than from the side of the board.

The whole game of chess, and the opening in particular, is like bartering with your opponent.

The king is always safest behind pawns left on the second rank (they are as far from the opponent's pieces as possible) and away from open files.

You should always try to play your pieces to good central posts in one move. Never spend two or three moves on one piece at the expense of the rest of your pieces unless you are forced to do so.

Chapter Two

The Middlegame: General Principles

- What should I attack?
- Where should I attack?
- What is a Weakness?
- What is a 'Good Square'?

In every game of chess, there are moments when a lifetime seems to be packed into a few moves: pieces are captured, structures destroyed and what remains is unrecognisable from the original scenario. It's as if a bomb has gone off on the chessboard! However, in order for these moments to occur, there inevitably have to be quieter periods leading up to them; periods when both sides mass and mobilise their pieces, looking to reach the posts from which to launch their attacks.

Having been a chessplayer for many years, there are some things which feel so natural to me that I never really consciously think about them during the game. It is those aspects of the game, however, that are always the most crucial for players who are just starting out. It's the stuff that helps you to make sense of chess: What should I attack? Where should I attack? What is a weakness? What is a 'good square' for a piece?

What should I attack?

The basic aim of the game is to checkmate the opponent's king. We all know this: it's in every book... and it's true! But it can give you the wrong impression of what you should be trying to do during a game. The crucial point is that *our aim is to checkmate the opponent's king **eventually***.

There is more than one way of defeating your opponent: the launch of a direct, violent attack, sacrificing a handful of pieces along the way, is the most spectacular, and usually the quickest method, but it is the exception to the rule. The normal path to victory is to win some of the opponent's pieces and thus to have more pieces than your opponent. Eventually you may aim to reach a position where the opponent only has his king while you have several pieces: then you checkmate him.

This is a very important point because it helps to answer the next question.

Where should I attack?

Where your opponent is weakest! If your opponent's king is exposed with nothing to defend it, as in the following diagram... (see diagram 1)

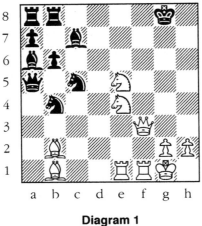

Diagram 1
The black king lacks cover

...then go for it: get the guy! However, if your opponent has for-tified his kingside at the expense of his queenside then don't hit him where he is strongest, just because his king is there. Go for the weakest target – his queenside – and take the sec-ond method of winning. Whenever you think about what you want to do, you shouldn't automatically think 'Right his king is over there, that's where all my pieces have to be!' You should try to think 'Where do I stand the best chance of achieving suc-cess – on the kingside or on the queenside?'

 TIP: Attack in the area of the board where your opponent is most vulnerable.

What is a Weakness?

There are three factors that you can apply when weighing up whether something is a weakness or not:

1. The soundness of the pawn structure
2. The ratio of attacking pieces compared to defending pieces
3. How easy it is to attack the target

The first of these factors is the most important skill for im-proving players.

Pawn Structure

In the beginning, both sides have a 'perfect', unblemished

structure (see diagram 2). It almost seems a shame to disturb it... but you have to! You have to move pawns to allow your bishops to develop. You have to gain space in order to put pressure on the opponent's position. As I keep stressing, chess is a game of balance. With every move you make, you gain things but you also have to give up some things as well. What does this mean?

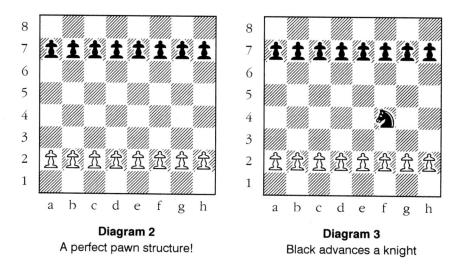

Diagram 2
A perfect pawn structure!

Diagram 3
Black advances a knight

Weak Squares and Outposts

From the starting position, let's play

1 e4

A good central pawn move, occupying the e4-square and attacking the d5-square. What could possibly be wrong with it? Nothing is *bad* about this move. However, once you play it, you automatically take away some things from your position that will never return. For example, 1 e4 slightly weakens White's protection of the f4- and d4-squares. How is that? Well with the pawn on e2, if a black knight came to f4 for example (see diagram 3) then White had two ways of driving it away: e2-e3 and g2-g3. After 1 e4, White only has one left. This is still enough at the moment, but say that after

1...e5

White played

2 g4? (see diagram 4)

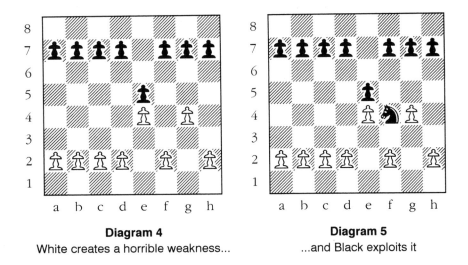

Diagram 4
White creates a horrible weakness...

Diagram 5
...and Black exploits it

Now the f4 square is terribly weak. Why? Because Black can later play a piece to this square (see diagram 5) and White will not be able to drive it away with a pawn.

Why is this so important? *Because in order to attack your opponent, you have to get close to his position.* It is often not too difficult to get the pieces where you want them, but it's keeping them there that is really hard. Once your pieces get close, they can be attacked by the opponent's pawns, and unless you have something brilliant they then have to retreat. In our example, with his first two moves, White has provided his opponent with an advanced square from which Black's pieces cannot be driven away by a pawn. This is what Black dreamed of – it is a very large concession. Unless White obtains something huge in return – and here he doesn't – he should not concede this square to his opponent.

This kind of principle can be used all over the board to show why certain combinations of pawn moves should be approached very carefully: d4 and f4 (see diagram 6) which concedes a good outpost on e4 for the black pieces, or ...h7-h5 and ...f7-f5 (see diagram 7) which create big weaknesses on g5 and g6.

What this means therefore is that when you play 1 e4, you reduce the chances of g2-g4 being a good move. This is not a terrible thing to concede, but... it's important to understand the thinking behind it.

diagram 14).

Compare this with diagram 15 when Black can win unassisted pawns much more quickly, e.g. 1...Re8 2 e5 Rd8 and there is no help for the pawn on d4.

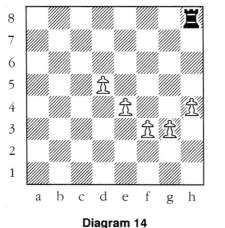

Diagram 14
Black has made no progress

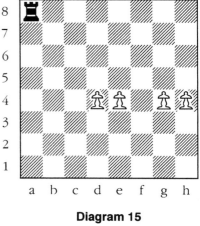

Diagram 15
The white pawns are vulnerable

TIP: Pawns are at their strongest when they are standing abreast in a continuous chain.

So let's now consider the most serious weakness: doubled pawns.

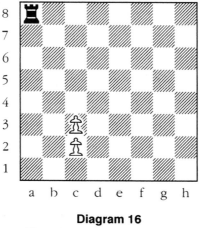

Diagram 16
The white pawns are easy prey

Here White's pawns cannot offer one another any support whatsoever – they are just cannon fodder for Black's rook.

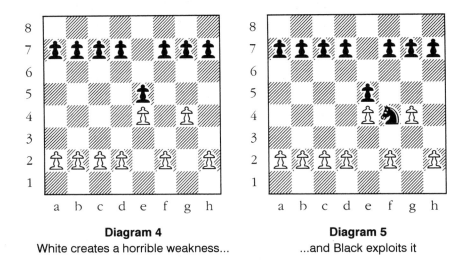

Diagram 4
White creates a horrible weakness...

Diagram 5
...and Black exploits it

Now the f4 square is terribly weak. Why? Because Black can later play a piece to this square (see diagram 5) and White will not be able to drive it away with a pawn.

Why is this so important? *Because in order to attack your opponent, you have to get close to his position.* It is often not too difficult to get the pieces where you want them, but it's keeping them there that is really hard. Once your pieces get close, they can be attacked by the opponent's pawns, and unless you have something brilliant they then have to retreat. In our example, with his first two moves, White has provided his opponent with an advanced square from which Black's pieces cannot be driven away by a pawn. This is what Black dreamed of – it is a very large concession. Unless White obtains something huge in return – and here he doesn't – he should not concede this square to his opponent.

This kind of principle can be used all over the board to show why certain combinations of pawn moves should be approached very carefully: d4 and f4 (see diagram 6) which concedes a good outpost on e4 for the black pieces, or ...h7-h5 and ...f7-f5 (see diagram 7) which create big weaknesses on g5 and g6.

What this means therefore is that when you play 1 e4, you reduce the chances of g2-g4 being a good move. This is not a terrible thing to concede, but... it's important to understand the thinking behind it.

WARNING: Be very careful of making pawn moves which create a 'hole' in your position.

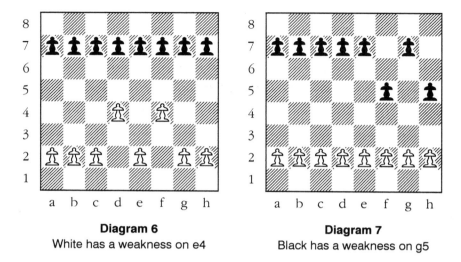

Diagram 6
White has a weakness on e4

Diagram 7
Black has a weakness on g5

Damaged Structures

When are pawns at their strongest?

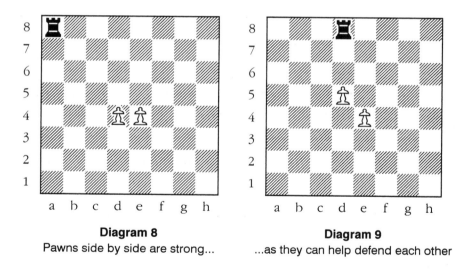

Diagram 8
Pawns side by side are strong...

Diagram 9
...as they can help defend each other

First of all, when they are side by side and able to support each other. For example, in diagram 8 the white pawns are able to help each other when attacked from the front. So 1...Re8 is met by 2 e5 (the pawn moves to where it is protected by the pawn on d4) and 1...Rd8 is met in the same vein by 2 d5 (see diagram 9). Contrast this with these other positions:

In diagram 10 the pawn on d4 is well protected, but after 1...Re8, the so-called 'backward' pawn on e3 is lost as the pawn on d4 cannot give it any support; and in diagram 11 the 'isolated' pawns provide each other with no support whatsoever, allowing Black to pick off whichever one he wants with 1...Rd8 or 1...Rf8. *or Ra4*

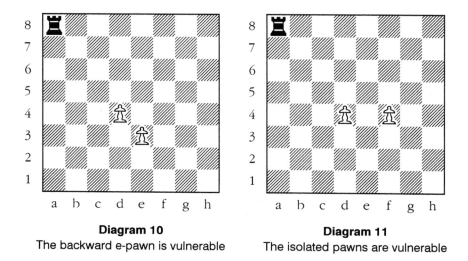

Diagram 10
The backward e-pawn is vulnerable

Diagram 11
The isolated pawns are vulnerable

Second, pawns are at their strongest when they form one continuous chain. For example in diagram 12 White's pawns can resist attack alone by themselves for a very long time:

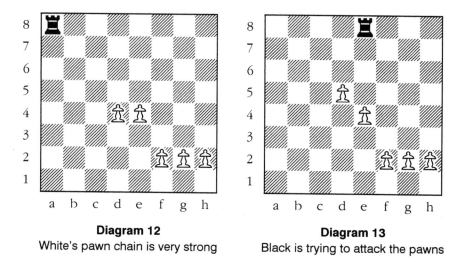

Diagram 12
White's pawn chain is very strong

Diagram 13
Black is trying to attack the pawns

1...Rd8 2 d5 Re8 (see diagram 13) 3 f3 Rg8 4 g3 Rh8 5 h4 (see

diagram 14).

Compare this with diagram 15 when Black can win unassisted pawns much more quickly, e.g. 1...Re8 2 e5 Rd8 and there is no help for the pawn on d4.

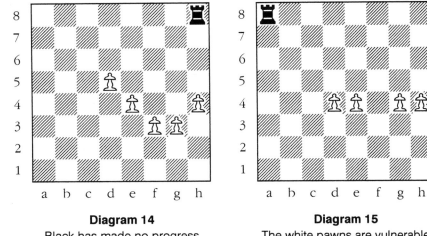

Diagram 14	Diagram 15
Diagram 14	**Diagram 15**
Black has made no progress	The white pawns are vulnerable

 TIP: Pawns are at their strongest when they are standing abreast in a continuous chain.

So let's now consider the most serious weakness: doubled pawns.

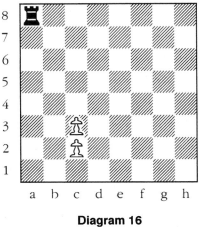

Diagram 16
The white pawns are easy prey

Here White's pawns cannot offer one another any support whatsoever – they are just cannon fodder for Black's rook.

The Ratio of Attacking Pieces to Defending Pieces

Thus far we have just concentrated on the most obvious form of weakness – pawn weaknesses. In real games, however, pieces also have something to say in the matter! In order for an area to be weak, the structure does not necessarily have to be damaged – it could be sound, but simply have a deficit of pieces to defend it:

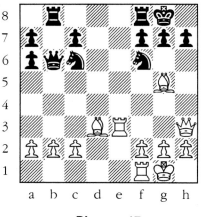

Diagram 17
Where is Black's weakness?

Here Black's queenside structure is fairly bad, but it is well covered by his pieces, so White cannot win anything there. However, Black's kingside is a huge weakness despite being completely untouched, because White has so many attacking pieces in that area – queen, rook and two bishops – and Black only has a knight on f6 to defend the king.

Long-term and Short-term Advantages

Look at the position in diagram 18:

White has a huge structural advantage and this is a *long-term advantage*. Why? Because whatever Black does, however many free moves you give him, Black can never alter the fact that White's pawns are linked and strong and Black's are isolated and weak. This factor will apply in the opening, the middlegame, and most of all in the endgame. But now go back to the previous diagram and look at White's piece superiority on the kingside – this is a *short-term advantage* because if you give

Black a few moves, he could bring some pieces over to the kingside in order to neutralise White's superiority in that area. It stands to reason therefore that *you need to cash in on a piece-based advantage much more quickly than you need to exploit a structural advantage.*

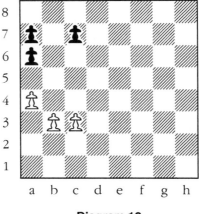

Diagram 18
White has a structural advantage

How Easy is it to attack the Target?

Top players don't break rules — what they do all the time, however, is to try to find the *exceptions* to individual rules in all types of positions — to push them to the limit, trying to get the very maximum out of every situation. This applies to every area of chess, but especially to the idea of structure. For example, let's take a look at a very topical line of the Sicilian Najdorf Defence that all the top players from Kasparov to Short are playing:

1 e4 c5 2 Nf3 d6 3 d4 cxd4 4 Nxd4 Nf6 5 Nc3 a6 6 Be3 e5 7 Nb3 Be6 (see diagram 19)

Black's sixth move seems to be completely against everything that I have said so far. First, the pawns on d6 and e5 are not standing abreast, which means that the pawn on e5 cannot give the pawn on d6 any support; and second, Black has conceded an advanced square on d5 to his opponent's pieces which Black cannot protect with a pawn. Have I been talking complete rubbish? No, both these things are true: they are the downside to Black's strategy, and they are the risks that Black takes when he plays this system. No, what the top players are doing is *disputing how serious the consequences are in this particular situation.* Let's ask a strong player about these two factors:

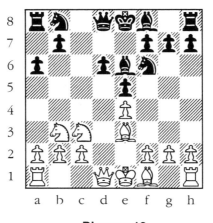

Diagram 19
Does Black have a weak spot on d5?

Q. Why did you allow a 'backward' pawn on d6?

A. 'OK, I agree, the d6-pawn is weak, but I can protect it easily with my dark-squared bishop. I don't think that White can put so much pressure on it that he can actually win it by force. So... then I can live with this, because while I'm accepting some disadvantages, I like the advantages that 6...e5 gave me.'

Q. But what about that weak square on d5?

A. 'Yes, this is a serious weakness, but I think it will only get bad for me if White can establish a piece there. *In this particular position*, I don't think that he can. For example, after 7...Be6, if White tries to put his knight on d5 with 8 Nd5 (see diagram 20) then Black is ready with 8...Bxd5! 9 exd5 (see diagram 21). Where is this great square for White's pieces now? Black has 'repaired' his structure by forcing a white pawn to d5.

'So, if White can't make use of this weakness immediately to harass me, then I can live with it! It's a risk I know, but I will take it because the benefits of 6...e5 are worthwhile in my opinion. And the benefits of 6...e5 are:

1. Black gains a good foothold in the centre, preventing White from using the d4- and f4-squares freely.

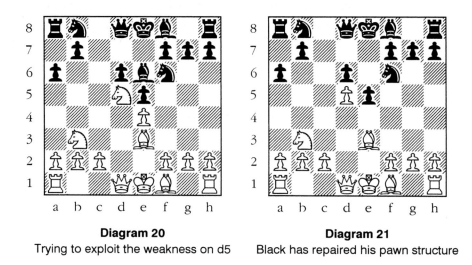

Diagram 20
Trying to exploit the weakness on d5

Diagram 21
Black has repaired his pawn structure

2. Black drives away the white knight on d4 from its central position, and with gain of tempo he

3. allows his king's bishop to develop to e7, thus preparing kingside castling, and

4. provides a post on e6 for his queen's bishop (it couldn't go there before because the knight on d4 was stopping it).'

Do these advantages outweigh the disadvantages? The debate goes on! Just remember that with all such arguments in chess, the general rules are not being disputed; the issue is whether there is another factor in the position that can justify the acceptance of such a weakness.

What is a 'Good Square' for a Piece?

We have already established a rough outline for where the pieces should generally go – towards the centre, and as close to the opponent's position as possible, in order to exert pressure and force concessions. We shall now go a little deeper into the differences between long-range and short-range pieces.

Rooks, Bishops And Queens

Rooks, bishops and queens are the *long-range pieces* – from the back rank on our side of the board, these pieces can attack targets in the opponent's position (see diagram 22). From the corner of the board the queen attacks the pawns on a7 and g7;

from the first rank, the rook on e1 attacks a knight on Black's back rank. From g2, White's light-squared bishop attacks a pawn on b7. But in contrast note the passivity of White's bishop on h2 and rook on h1, both of which are blocked by other pieces and have no influence on the game.

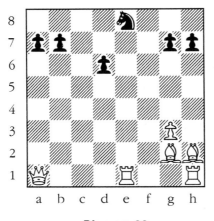

Diagram 22
The long-range pieces in action

TIP: Long-range pieces should be placed where nothing blocks them: on open files and diagonals. Also, long-range pieces will come into their own once there are fewer pawns and the position opens up.

So, going back to the Ruy Lopez position we saw earlier.

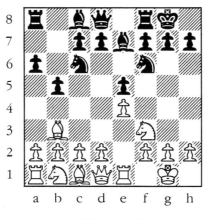

Diagram 23
The b3-bishop is on a good diagonal

Here it is clear that White has found an excellent diagonal for his light-squared bishop. From b3, it has a clear path down to the f7-pawn. Of all the long-range pieces, bishops are able to find good posts first because they are easily able to move away from behind the pawn chain. However, look at White's rooks and queen (and Black's too for that matter). They are not doing very much are they? Is that worrying? No! If all the pawns are on the board, the board is inevitably very crowded; there is simply no space for these big pieces to manoeuvre, so they have nothing to do for the moment. The aims of both sides will be to use the minor pieces (i.e. knights and bishops) and pawns to create gaps in the position that the 'big guys' can exploit with devastating effect. Talking of the role of minor pieces brings us to the most important piece in any form of manoeuvring: the knight.

Knights

The knight is a *short-range piece*. We can see this clearly if we add a couple of knights to our long-range diagram.

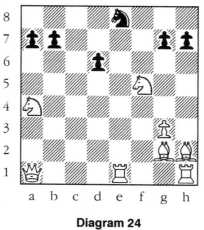

Diagram 24
Knights are short-range pieces

Only one knight has any real influence on the opponent's position – the one on f5. In other words, knights have to be closer than the other pieces in order to do any damage to the opponent's position. This inevitably means that you will normally have to spend more moves to transfer a knight to a good post than, for example, a bishop.

What is a Good Post for a Knight?

Most commonly, you aim to place a knight on an *outpost*; usually this is a central square (from where the knight attacks the most squares) where the knight is supported by a pawn.

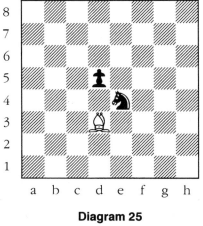

Diagram 25
Black's knight is well placed

Here the knight is protected by a pawn on d5. Though White's bishop attacks the knight, White is not threatening to win it. However, an outpost is only a good one if the knight cannot driven away by a pawn. For example, take a look at this slightly unusual variation of the Alekhine Defence:

1 e4 Nf6 2 Nc3 d5 3 e5 Ne4 4 Ne2!? (see diagram 26)

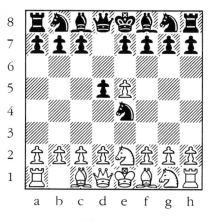

Diagram 26
The black knight can be driven away

White's last move is rather strange but he recognises that Black's outpost on e4 is not very permanent – White can easily drive the knight away from its outpost with d2-d3 (or f2-f3) on the next move.

This point should make us focus again on why you should be aware of the weaknesses you leave behind when advancing pawns. Let us go back to the Ruy Lopez again (see diagram 27).

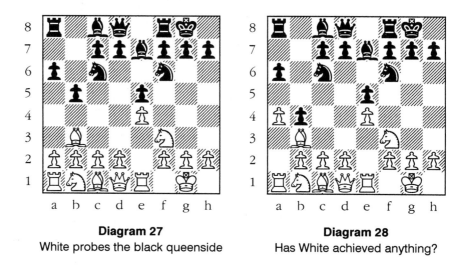

Diagram 27
White probes the black queenside

Diagram 28
Has White achieved anything?

I said that White had slightly unravelled Black's position by drawing out 6...b5 from him. I realise this probably didn't seem very clear at the time, but the presence of the pawn on b5 gives White a new chance to put pressure on Black's position with

8 a4

Well, if you put pressure on the opponent, he has to react: Black has to do something. Say he plays

8...b4 (see diagram 28)

Has White achieved anything?

What squares did the pawn attack when it was on b5? Obviously a4 and c4. What squares is it attacking now? a3 and c3. What squares can this pawn never attack again in its life? Okay, a4 and c4! Once a pawn has moved forward, it can never turn back towards home again. This means that if White puts a piece on the c4-square, it can now never be attacked by the black b-pawn – it is completely safe and is entrenched on that square. Obviously, Black could try to remove it by playing his d-pawn to d5, but in this position, it would just be exchanged by e4xd5. So what piece should we put on there? Well, how about a knight?

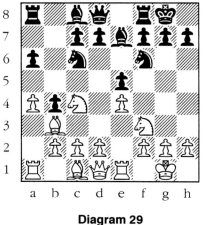

Diagram 29
c4 is a good square for the knight

From c4, the knight helps to put pressure on Black's e5-pawn while also attacking queenside squares. And, most importantly, the knight also has *prospects* on this square. From c4, it can then move later to e3 and then either to d5 or especially to f5, an outpost close to the black king. How does the knight get to c4? Well, White can play

9 d3 and then Nd2 and Nc4.

Good handling of the knights is one of the most important positional skills. Part of this skill is being able to see instantly a path for your knights to reach good squares – after you identify a good outpost, it is really important to be able to work out how to get them there! So I want to show you an exercise that I do myself to help develop this. It can be fun to do with someone else as well.

Try it Yo

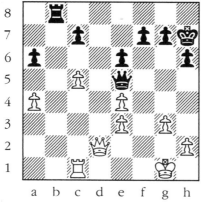

nd put place black pawns
e d3, e5, f6, h2. Now take a
s on the board – one will be
other will be the square
)ut in your head the quick-
hat the knight can take,
a black pawn. You're not
r! When you think you've
got it, play it out on the board and see if you're right. If there is
more than one route of the same number of moves, then note
both of them. Practising like this just five minutes a day will
really help you to see where knights can go in practical games.

Exercise 2 Assess this position.

Exercise 3 What sort of advantages do both sides possess?

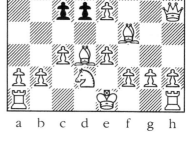

Exercise 2   Exercise 3

Summary

Attack where your opponent is weakest!

In order to attack your opponent, you have to get your pieces close to his position.

Pawns are at their strongest when they are standing abreast in a continuous chain.

You need to cash in on a piece-based advantage much more quickly than you need to exploit a structural advantage

Long-range pieces will come into their own once there are fewer pawns and the position opens up.

Chapter Three

Middlegame Tactics

- 'The Toe-Bone is connected to the Foot-Bone...'
- 'Something is worrying Me...!'
- 'My Position is full of Holes!'

So much of chess is a struggle between the general and the specific. Both sides try to implement general principles, but each attempts to derail the other's plans by attempting to show that what is normally correct is not the best in *these specific circumstances.* We saw this first of all in the Ruy Lopez (see diagram 1) when the good general move 6...0-0 loses a pawn to 7 Bxc6 dxc6 8 Nxe5. We then saw it again in the Najdorf – the 'illogical' 6...e5 (see diagram 2). Black willingly accepts a backward pawn on d6 and a weak square on d5.

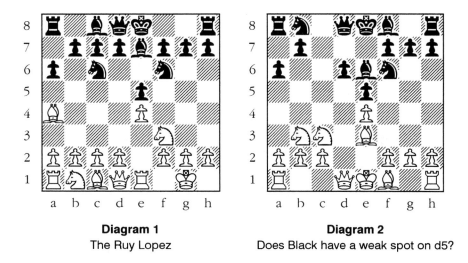

<table>
<tr><td>**Diagram 1**</td><td>**Diagram 2**</td></tr>
<tr><td>The Ruy Lopez</td><td>Does Black have a weak spot on d5?</td></tr>
</table>

The latter is an extremely complicated example, but the first is very close to everyday experience. It is not enough to understand the general principles. You also need to work out whether they can be implemented in a straightforward manner, or whether an obstacle exists which requires a specific solution. Compare it to crossing a busy street – you have to know where you want to go, but in the short-term, the most important thing is to watch out for all those speeding cars and lorries!

It is impossible to list all the traps and tricks in chess – there are far too many! What I want to discuss in this chapter are the *warning signs*. These are the things that should make you sit up and take notice when you spot them in a position, whether or not you see a specific way in which they can be exploited. *It is absolutely crucial to develop a good **sense of danger**.* There is nothing more frustrating than messing up a good game by missing a trick at the end. A good sense of danger will also speed up your thinking process and make it more efficient: it is so tiring to spend time working out a move, only to realise just before you play it that it loses a piece or allows your opponent to take your queen. You have to notice these things immediately!

'The Toe-Bone is connected to the Foot-Bone...'

Although chess positions can sometimes look like a random assortment of pieces, *in every position there are links and 'relationships' between pieces.* When the position is very quiet and there is no danger it is easy to forget about these links, but they become crucial when the position explodes. Let's go back once again to the Ruy Lopez position after move eight (see diagram 3).

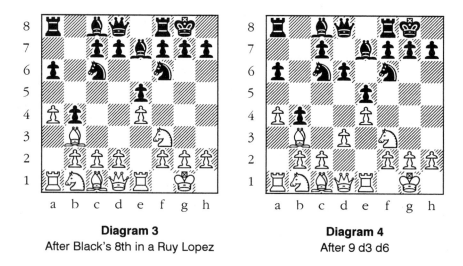

Diagram 3
After Black's 8th in a Ruy Lopez

Diagram 4
After 9 d3 d6

There are several obvious 'friendships' within the position: the white rook on e1 protects the pawn on e4; the black knight on c6 is the sole defender of the e5-pawn; and this black knight also defends the pawn on b4 in combination with the bishop on e7. As further moves are played, these relationships are constantly being altered slightly. Often there are no immediate consequences, but it really helps to keep track of them so that you never make the mistake of assuming that something is defended when in fact you left it undefended a few moves before!

How does this work in practice? Well let's play a few more

moves and see:

9 d3

The pawn on e4 is now defended by a pawn, which alters the relationship between the pawn on e4 and the rook on e1. The rook will now be able to move from e1 later if it wishes.

9...d6 (see diagram 4)

Black protects his pawn on e5 with his d-pawn and relieves his knight on c6 from this duty. But just as one door is opened, another closes: the pawn on b4 is now no longer defended by the bishop on e7 – 9...d6 closes the f8-a3 diagonal – so the pawn is now defended only once. This has no immediate significance as White is showing no interest in the pawn. At the moment, it would not matter even if it were not defended at all, but it is a good example of how normal moves have consequences that are easy to overlook, and if we are not aware of them, it is easy to give away something carelessly at a later point in the game!

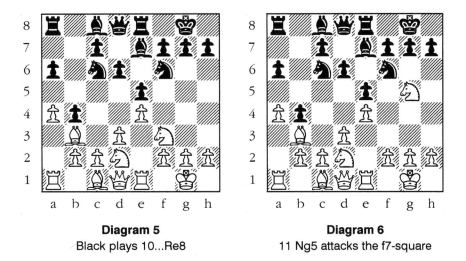

Diagram 5
Black plays 10...Re8

Diagram 6
11 Ng5 attacks the f7-square

10 Nbd2

White continues to develop and prepares to transfer his knight to the good square c4.

10...Re8 (see diagram 5)

A normal move, but which relationship does this alter? Well, the pawn on f7, which was attacked by the bishop on b3 and defended by the king on g8 and rook on f8, is now defended only by the king on g8. Black's natural move has reduced the defence of one of his pawns. So if White now plays

11 Ng5 (see diagram 6)

increasing the attack on the pawn, there is a big threat of Nxf7 or Bxf7+ winning a pawn and wrecking Black's position.

 WARNING: Keep your sense of danger by observing which pieces are protecting or covering other pieces. Be aware when those relationships are changed.

When the position is quiet, the interaction between the pieces is less important. However, when the position becomes more open, with more space for the pieces to move into offensive positions, it is then that this becomes a vital 'survival skill'.

'Something is worrying Me...!'

In order to lose material, something somewhere has to be attacked. This is an extremely obvious thing to say, but you should use it to reduce the number of things you have to worry about! You should look for danger in the areas where your opponent has pressure. So in this position as Black (see diagram 7) you would look for danger on the kingside, but not really on the queenside. I stress this merely because the board can sometimes be so confusing that you expect disaster to strike in any and every quarter and you just spend all your thinking time worrying rather than finding a solution to your problems!

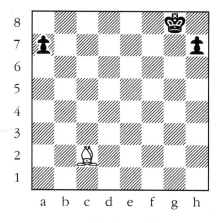

Diagram 7
The white bishop eyes the black kingside

In open positions, danger stems from a target being attacked and then defended (see diagram 8).

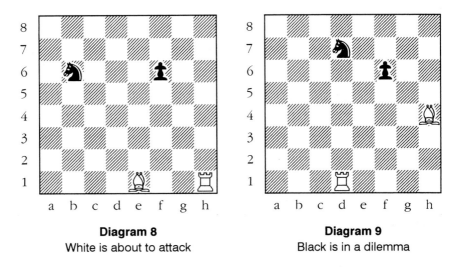

Diagram 8
White is about to attack

Diagram 9
Black is in a dilemma

1 Bh4 attacks the pawn on f6. **1...Nd7** defends it. However, a new relationship has formed in the position, that of the knight on d7 and the pawn on f6. The knight on d7 has a new little friend to take care of! The knight must remain on d7, tied to the pawn on f6 because the pawn's life depends upon it. And when there is such an obligation within a position, it's the opponent's duty to make it very hard to fulfil!

Picture the scene... the pawn is really scared but for the moment it's breathing easier because it knows the knight will take the bishop if the bishop does anything to it! But then the bishop's friend, the rook, comes along and attacks the knight... **2 Rd1** (see diagram 9).

What is the knight to do? If it stays where it is, the rook will capture it; if it moves then the bishop will capture its friend. There is nothing that Black can do – he must lose either a piece or a pawn, and all because White was able to put pressure on his opponent's position, creating a dependency within it which led to disaster.

This is not to put you off protecting your pieces when they are attacked! However, it is this factor – forcing pieces to cover each other, tying them down with 'responsibilities' to each other and thus reducing their ability to move around freely –

that is the basis for most tactical tricks and combinations.

Do you want to see how it looks in a game situation? Okay!

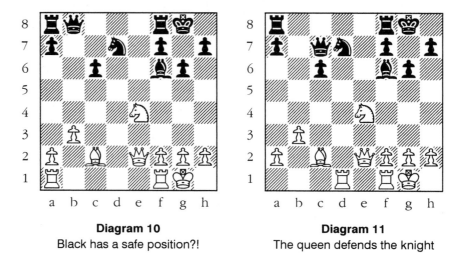

Diagram 10
Black has a safe position?!

Diagram 11
The queen defends the knight

Black's position is diagram 10 doesn't look so bad does it? His king looks safe and his bishop on f6 is even attacking White's rook on a1. But is there anything 'suspicious' in Black's position? Hmm, well the bishop on f6 is attacked by White's knight on e4, and it is only defended by the knight on d7. If the knight on d7 has to move, then White will simply be able to take the bishop... Aha, the bishop on f6 doesn't want to see that knight leave d7 – Black's position kind of depends on that link remaining... Hmm, so what if I attack the knight on d7 with...

1 Rad1

If it moves, I just take the bishop and I'm a piece up! But what if Black plays

1...Qc7 (see diagram 11)

protecting the knight, what then? Well, let's think. The knight is defending the bishop, but if it were no longer there... Well, then I could just take the bishop with my knight... Right, so if I play

2 Rxd7

then I lose out first of all because a rook is a bit less valuable than a knight, but after

2...Qxd7 (see diagram 12)

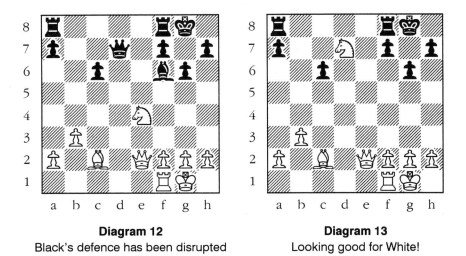

Diagram 12
Black's defence has been disrupted

Diagram 13
Looking good for White!

I can just play

3 Nxf6+

and take another piece while Black can take nothing back. So the overall count is two pieces for a rook for me which is definitely in my favour! *And,* as a huge bonus in this position, I've just noticed that the knight on f6 is forking the king on g8 and the queen on d7! By deflecting the queen to the d7-square, I've made sure that as well as capturing the bishop, I'm going to win the queen for nothing as well!

3...Kg7 4 Nxd7 (see diagram 13)

Now I'm really happy!

TIP: When pieces are attacked, but only defended once, this opens up many combinational possibilities

With every variation of this basic theme, the principle and the starting point are the same: whether you are the World Champion or the most inexperienced beginner, you must notice the relationship between the knight and the bishop before you can even think of the combination. This first step has to be taken; only then will you be able to take the right action. The principle of noticing relationships and exploiting them also applies to something else: pieces and squares.

'My Position is full of Holes!'

Pieces not only defend each other; they also defend empty squares.

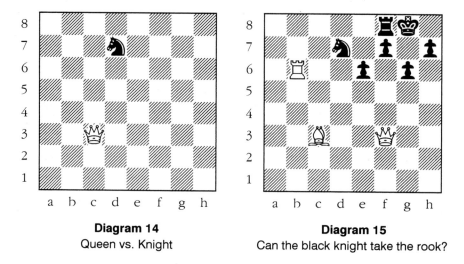

Diagram 14
Queen vs. Knight

Diagram 15
Can the black knight take the rook?

Although the queen is much more powerful than the knight, in diagram 14 the queen knows that if she moves to c5 or to f6 or to e5, she will be taken with no regard shown for her elevated position in society. This is obviously a powerful defensive resource and you can imagine that single pieces, or even pawns, can be crucial defensive pieces if they guard squares that must not be invaded by the opponent. In this case, an obligation exists between piece and squares, as it did between piece and pawn or piece and piece in our previous examples. It may seem strange, but *it isn't only the physical things in your position – the pieces and pawns – that you have to defend, but also the empty space within it!* It is harder to spot this, of course, but the obligation and the relationship is just as real.

Take a look at this example (see diagram 15): Black's kingside dark squares are rather vulnerable (if only he had a dark-squared bishop on g7!) but the knight on d7 controls the f6-square and prevents any disaster. But if Black gets tempted by the rook on b6 and plays **1...Nxb6** then after **2 Qf6!** Black cannot prevent checkmate on g7 or h8. The knight had an obligation to the f6-square as surely as if a piece was on that square; once the knight relinquished its responsibility, disaster ensued.

Try it Yourself

From each of the following positions, a sequence of moves will be played. During this, one side will give the other a chance to pounce! It could be either White or Black, so be vigilant – your task is to point out where the opportunity was missed.

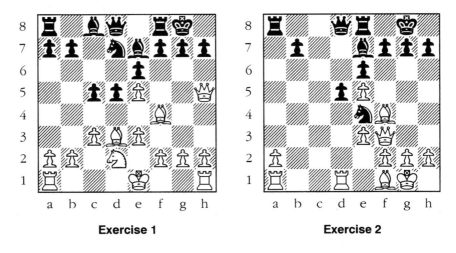

Exercise 1   Exercise 2

Exercise 1: 1...c4 2 Bc2 Nc5 Aiming for the d3-square. **3 b3 Nd3+ 4 Bxd3 cxd3**.

Exercise 2: 1 h3 A useful move avoiding future back-rank mates. **1...Qa5 2 Rab1** Attacking the loose pawn on b7. **2...Ra7** Black defends it and prepares to double his rooks on the a-file against the isolated white pawn on a2. **3 Rb5 Qc7**.

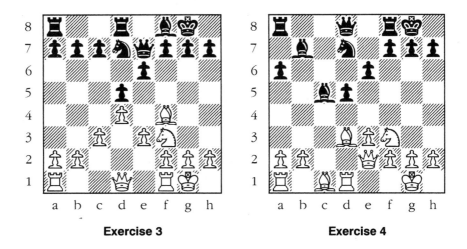

Exercise 3   Exercise 4

Exercise 3: 1...c5 Black puts pressure on the white centre. **2 Re1** White prepares a central push of his own: e3-e4. **2...Rc8** Good steady development by Black. This is a quiet position and there is nothing dramatic for him to do. His queen's rook is more active on c8 than on a8 so he plays it there. **3 Qd3 Qf6** Black brings his queen to the kingside **4 Ng5 g6!** Saw that one! **5 e4** White breaks in the centre! **5...cxd4 6 cxd4 Nb6**.

Exercise 4: 1 a3 White wants to expand on the queenside with b2-b4. I would have preferred to develop my queenside more modestly with 1 b3 followed by 2 Bb2. **1...Nb6** An interesting move: Black anticipates that after White's next move **2 b4 Be7** White will have queenside holes on the a4- and c4-squares. From b6, the knight is ideally-placed to exploit them both. **3 Bb2 Bf6** To neutralise White's well-placed dark-squared bishop on b2.

Summary

Chess is a struggle between the general and the specific.

It is absolutely crucial to develop a good sense of danger.

In every position there are links and 'relationships' between pieces.

The way to keep your sense of danger is to notice which pieces are protecting or covering other pieces, and to be aware when those relationships are changed.

It isn't only the physical things in your position – the pieces and pawns – that you have to defend, but also the empty space within it!

Chapter Four

Endgame Principles

- 'We're Outnumbered, Boys...'
- What is the Aim of the Endgame?
- Thinking Longer-Term
- Evaluating Endgames

The endgame is the part of the game that scares everyone, beginner and grandmaster alike. Everybody knows how important it is to be a good endgame player – the endgame is your final chance to save a lost position, or your last hope to win a better position – but everybody is really afraid that they aren't actually very effective in the endgame!

I know this sounds very strange. When I was teaching her to play chess, my mother always said that as there are fewer pieces on the board, shouldn't the endgame be a lot simpler than the opening or the middlegame? There are fewer threats to worry about, fewer pieces that can fork you, fewer pieces of your own that you can forget about and leave unprotected! This is actually the fundamental question – once you understand why the endgame is far from simple, then you will understand the general attitude you should adopt for the endgame.

'We're Outnumbered, Boys...'

Although it is easy to lose track of things in the middlegame, the great thing about having plenty of pieces, is that there always seems to a piece spare to defend your position when it is suddenly attacked. *In the ending, however, your forces are much reduced but you still have the same area of territory to cover* – it's like an army having to hold the same strip of territory but with a quarter of the forces you had before. Inevitably, weaknesses are harder to cover and it is harder to attack the opponent's position in order to distract him from attacking you.

Usually in the middlegame, you need something clever – such as a move that attacks two pieces at the same time – in order to win material. In the endgame, a simple, uncomplicated attack on a pawn can just lead to a winning position. For example (see diagram 1)

White plays **1 Bd2** winning a pawn and the game.

This is a very simple easy move – but Black can do nothing about it! In the middlegame, Black would always have a piece to spare for defensive duties, but in the endgame you start to run out of pieces! So in contrast to the middlegame, where there is a constant flow of little attacks to spot, in the endgame there are less of these on every move because the firepower on both sides is much reduced. However, when attacks do actually occur they can be absolutely devastating, and may even finish the game off in one move.

Diagram 1
A simple endgame

I always compare the middlegame and the endgame in my mind as the difference between navigating a speedboat and an oil tanker. In the middlegame, your position is 'speedy' and manoeuvrable: you can deal with threats on both sides of the board, change plans and go from one side of the board to the other at a moment's notice. In the endgame your position is slow and cumbersome – if you place all your pieces on one side, you will not be able to get back quickly to deal with the problems on the other side. You have to choose your direction carefully because once you start, you will not be able to alter it easily. As you can see, you need to have a rather different attitude in order to play the endgame successfully, compared to the middlegame.

What is the Aim of the Endgame?

Of course, the aim of the endgame is the same as in all of chess: to checkmate the opponent's king. However, the rider that I put in the middlegame section is even more pertinent here: the aim is to checkmate the opponent's king *eventually*. Obviously, with fewer attacking pieces and more free space on the board, *you are much less likely to have a mating attack against the king*. Take a look at these examples:

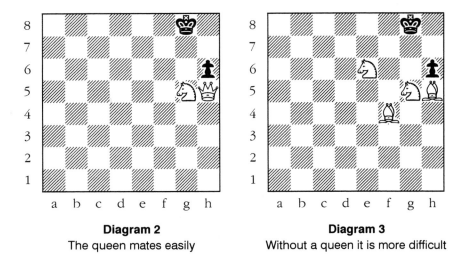

Diagram 2
The queen mates easily

Diagram 3
Without a queen it is more difficult

With the queen on the board (see diagram 2), White mates easily with **1 Qf7+ Kh8 2 Qh7 checkmate.** Two pieces, easy! Without queens on the board (see diagram 3), White needs masses of material in order to cover all the escape squares available to the black king: **1 Bf7+ Kh8 2 Be5 checkmate**.

So mating attacks in the endgame are going to be very rare. So how on earth can you win if you are going to find it hard to checkmate the opponent with the pieces that you have? Simple, you need reinforcements – you need to queen a pawn!

Queening a Pawn

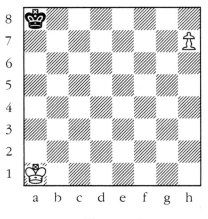

Diagram 4
Queening a pawn

This is the 'magical' factor in chess – the factor that can turn even the slightest material advantage into a win. By themselves, the white king and pawn have no chance of checkmating the black king – they can't restrict it, or force it to do anything he doesn't want to do. But after...**1 h8Q+** (see diagram 4) ...suddenly everything has changed! The queen will restrict and pin down the black king, and together the white king and queen can easily deliver checkmate on the black king. So the aim in the ending is the same as in all of chess – to *eventually* checkmate the opponent's king. In the ending, though, you have an extra step before you can do this: you have to recharge the level of your forces; and you do this by getting one of your pawns to the eighth rank. This raises some important observations: *It is very important to realise just how huge is the difference made by changing a pawn into a queen.* When a pawn turns into a queen on the eighth rank, you're getting a Rolls-Royce for your toy bike. Your position becomes 100 times better! Consequently, you should always be aware of possibilities of sacrificing material – a piece or even two pieces – so that in a couple of moves' time, you can queen a pawn.

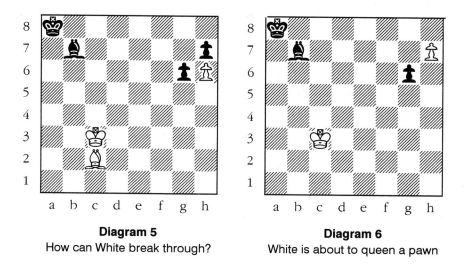

Diagram 5
How can White break through?

Diagram 6
White is about to queen a pawn

In diagram 5 White can play **1 Bxg6! hxg6** Yes, White is a piece down, a whole piece down... but he's winning! **2 h7** (see diagram 6). Now Black cannot stop the h-pawn from queening. **2...g5 3 h8Q+** and suddenly the position is transformed – a queen appears on the board and it is clear that White has a won game.

'The Stone that the Builders rejected has become the Capstone...'

In the middlegame, it's the pieces that command all the attention, with their long-range threats and daring manoeuvres. Pawns only seem to be there as victims, or as a gauge of how things are going – 'I'm two pawns up so I must be winning.'

In the ending, however, the pawn's ability to be transformed into the most powerful piece on the board means that the health and strength of the pawns on both sides suddenly becomes the most crucial factor on the board. This amazing change – the least becoming the first – is indicative of the general mood you need for the ending. All the 'quiet' things – structure, planning, pawns – that can easily be overshadowed in the middlegame by the 'noise' of heavy pieces hurling themselves everywhere, suddenly come into life in the endgame. In a way, you have to 'listen' harder to the position. You have to really try to assess it accurately, because you can't use your large arsenal of big pieces to confuse the issue and get you out of trouble.

Thinking Longer-Term

I keep stressing the importance of thinking very long-term in the endgame. In the middlegame, it is very difficult to do this. Never believe anyone who says that grandmasters routinely plan 20-30 moves ahead! Sometimes in the middlegame, you can have a general feel for where things might go, but there is simply too much potential for the unpredictable to happen to be able to have such a clear idea of what lies ahead. However, in the endgame, with so few pieces, there is a lot less interference with your plans. You can say, 'I want my king to go there' and carry it out, because the opponent does not have the resources to stop you. In those sort of circumstances, it is easily possible to draw up a plan of several stages lasting 20-30 moves. This is a very important point to understand.

 NOTE: In the endgame it is often possible to draw up a plan that lasts for 20 or 30 moves.

'I don't believe it! It was losing all along!'

Sometimes in the endgame a position can be lost for you from a very 'long way back'. In the middlegame, with so many pieces to cloud the issue, positions are only completely hopelessly lost a few moves from the end. But in the endgame, the position can reach this stage many moves earlier, before it even looks that bad! What do I mean? Well, take a look at this example:

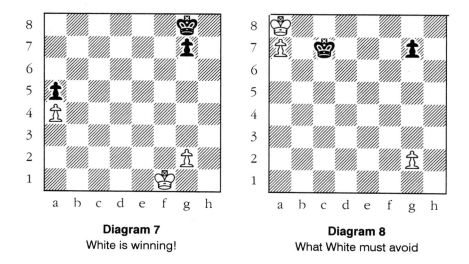

Diagram 7
White is winning!

Diagram 8
What White must avoid

Diagram 7 doesn't look appalling for Black, does it? Same material, the only slight difference being that White's king is a tiny bit closer to the centre than Black's, but such a small difference can't mean anything, right? *Wrong*! This position is completely lost for Black – he has no hope whatsoever of saving the game... and I can tell you exactly how it will happen!

White will play his king to the a5-pawn and win it. Black has two possibilities:

Scenario 1: While White wins the a5 pawn, Black takes his king to the g2-pawn to win it and tries to queen his own pawn. However, White is much quicker!

Scenario 2: Black follows the white king to the a5-pawn and tries to keep the white king boxed in to reach the type of position in diagram 8.

This would be a draw: Black can keep the white king boxed in for as long as he needs to by oscillating between c7 and c8. However, White will not go forward with his king, but back and use his a-pawn as a decoy. While the black king is dealing with the a-pawn, White's king will run over to the black g-pawn, capture it and then shepherd his own pawn to queen. Want to see all this in action? Okay!

Scenario 1

1 Ke2 Kf7 2 Kd3 Kg6 3 Kc4 Kg5 4 Kb5 Kg4 5 Kxa5 Kg3 6 Kb4 Kxg2 7 a5 g5 8 a6 g4 9 a7 g3 10 a8Q+ which is a win for White as we shall see: **10...Kh2 11 Kc3 g2 12 Qh8+** White's aim is to get his queen closer to the pawn and by checks to force the black king to occupy g1 – the square in front of the pawn. When this happens, the pawn cannot advance to queen, which gives White an opportunity to get his king closer. White can repeat this process indefinitely until the white king is close enough to help the queen give mate. It take a lot of moves, but there is *nothing* that Black can do about it. **12...Kg3 13 Qg7+ Kf2 14 Qf6+ Ke2 15 Qg5** ...getting closer all the time. **15...Kf2 16 Qf4+ Ke2 17 Qg3 Kf1 18 Qf3+!** (see diagram 9) Here it is: if the black king moves to e1, then White simply captures the g2-pawn. So the king has to move to g1, but then... **18...Kg1 19 Kd2!** ...getting closer still. **19...Kh2 20 Qf2 Kh1 21 Qh4+! Kg1 22 Ke3!** Not 22 Ke2?? *stalemate!* **22...Kf1 23 Qf2 checkmate** (see diagram 10).

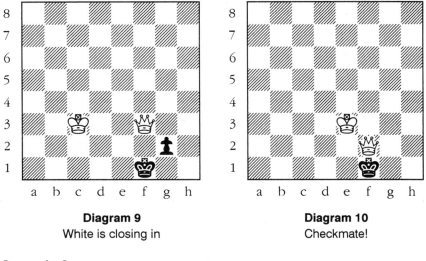

Diagram 9
White is closing in

Diagram 10
Checkmate!

Scenario 2

1 Ke2 Kf7 2 Kd3 Ke6 3 Kc4 Kd6 4 Kb5 Kd5 5 Kxa5 Kc5 6 g4 White sensibly advances the pawn that will eventually queen closer to the queening square – every little helps! **6...g5**

7 Ka6 Kc6 8 a5 Kc7 9 Kb5! The king now heads for the king-side. Black can't follow the white king over there straightaway or the a-pawn will queen. First of all, Black must deal with the a-pawn before chasing the white king, and this costs him too much time. **9...Kb7 10 Kc5 Ka6 11 Kd5 Kxa5 12 Ke5 Kb5 13 Kf5 Kc6 14 Kxg5 Kd7 15 Kf6 Ke8 16 Kg7!** White prevents the black king from occupying the queening square and thus prepares to move his pawn forward without hindrance.
16...Ke7 17 g5 Ke8 18 g6 Ke7 19 Kh7! Now the king makes way for the pawn. **19...Kf6 20 g7 Kf7 21 g8Q+** and White will win shortly.

That took a lot of moves, but there was no hope whatsoever for Black of changing events by his own efforts – only great care-lessness from White could possibly save Black from defeat. This kind of long drawn-out winning procedure could not happen in a middlegame, but it frequently arises in the endgame. This raises an important subject.

Simplifying the Position as a Winning Tool

Attempts to win in the middlegame are always fraught with danger – you might get caught in a mating attack, or you might miss something and drop a piece. However, winning in the endgame, as we saw from the position above, is much simpler. It may take a long time, but the moves are not too diffi-cult – it's just like filling in your personal details on a form: you mustn't be careless, but if you concentrate, you can do it right 100 times out of 100. So, if you are material up, or if you can reach an ending like the one in the previous example, where the crucial advantages are in your favour, this is the best percentage way of converting your advantage. What we now have to look at is how to judge whether an ending is good or not.

Evaluating Endgames

Evaluation in the ending uses the same basic mechanism that we saw for evaluating weaknesses in the middlegame. The im-portant difference however is that static factors – pawn struc-ture, etc. – are absolutely crucial in endings, whereas in mid-dlegames they can sometimes be 'hidden' by active factors.

Static Factors

In the middlegame, the large number of pieces can swarm around the board, creating noise and activity, distracting you, blinding you so that you are unable to see clearly your opponent's weaknesses. For example:

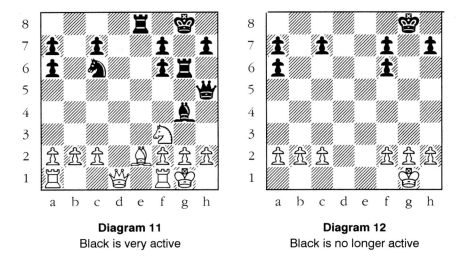

Diagram 11
Black is very active

Diagram 12
Black is no longer active

In diagram 11 Black has a horrible structure with two sets of doubled pawns, but because of the pieces around White's king, White has no time to even think of exploiting them. However, take away Black's activity and... (see diagram 12) you have a truly disgusting ending for Black!

In endings, static weaknesses become much clearer, no excuses can be made for them, no factors found to compensate fully for them. So when assessing endings, the first thing you should do is to understand whose structure is the stronger, and you should place a great deal of importance on this.

Damaged structures are particularly bad in the ending because they are easier to attack and because it is much harder to create a queen with them! For example in diagram 13 White has a 2-1 pawn majority on the kingside and Black has a 2-1 pawn majority on the queenside. However, whereas the white pawns can create a passed pawn on the kingside, Black's pawns are doubled – he can't do anything on the queenside. White's one pawn there is a complete match for Black's two pawns. White is essentially a pawn up, and is completely winning in fact.

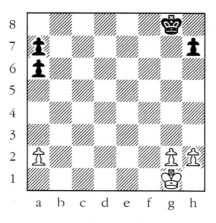

Diagram 13
Level material but White wins

As we have said before, good pawns are sheer gold dust in the ending! The importance of the pawn structure leads to another important factor in the endgame.

The Relationship between Pieces and Pawns

Unfortunately, although pawns are *potentially* the most powerful pieces on the board, and must thus be protected carefully, they are still the same limited unit before they reach the eighth rank, unable to defend properly against attack. *Thus the weaker the pawns, the less active the pieces in the ending.* Unlike in the middlegame the pieces cannot organise an attack on the king to keep the opponent's eyes away from their pawn structure, so they have to take defensive roles to hold their pawns or concede a material disadvantage.

 WARNING: Poor pawn structure leads to poor pieces in the endgame.

In diagram 14 White's pieces attack his opponent's weaknesses on e6 and a6 and keep the bishop passive on c8.

However, note that if you moved Black's pawn on a7 to b5, and Black's pawn on e6 to f7 you would 'repair' Black's structure considerably. But Black's structure would still be 'bad' because the pawn on a6 has to be defended by the bishop on c8 due to the attack on it by the knight on c5. We thus see another type of weakness – the bad piece that fits in badly with the structure. A further example is seen in diagram 15.

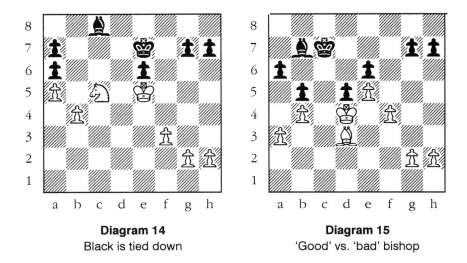

Diagram 14
Black is tied down

Diagram 15
'Good' vs. 'bad' bishop

This is a typical 'good' vs. 'bad' bishop situation. White's bishop is on the opposite colour to most of its pawns so it can move freely; whereas Black's is restricted by all of those pawns on light squares. It has no active squares because they are all blocked by its own pawns. The corollary to this is that Black has virtually no control over any of his dark squares in his position. If you have no real control over 50% of the squares in your territory, then you are obviously going to suffer.

Active Factors

The most important active factor in an ending is one that does not even arise in the middlegame: the activity of the king. As we have seen, the king is a very mobile and dangerous piece in the endgame. Freed from the threat of being checkmated, it can wander across the board in search of weaknesses. Its great strength is its ability to attack weaknesses on squares of any colour, which means that no weakness is safe from a king. So important is this factor that, as we saw in diagram 7, a slight difference in activity can make a huge difference to the outcome of the game. In general, the nearer to the centre the king is, the more active it is. This is not to say that the king must always be brought to the centre (if the centre is closed and all the action is on the kingside, for example, that would make no sense!). However, from the centre, the king is never likely to be too far away from trouble-spots on either wing.

Try it Yourself

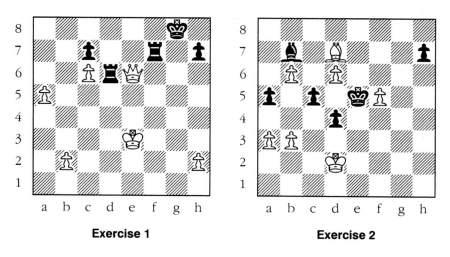

Exercise 1   **Exercise 2**

Exercise 1: This is a position from Sadler-Benjamin, National Club Championship 1987. White to play and queen a pawn!

Exercise 2: This is from my game against Michael Adams at a tournament in London in 1989. There was an immediate win here that I missed. Can you queen one of my pawns for me?

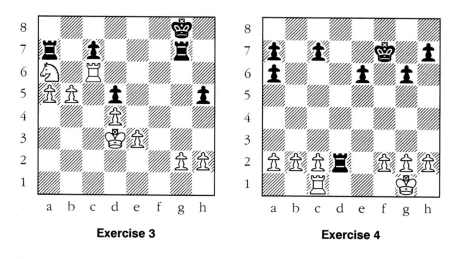

Exercise 3   **Exercise 4**

Exercise 3: Again, I have a chance to make a queen, this time against Geenen in Metz 1989. Go for it!

Exercise 4: a) Assess this position; and b) Move the white rook to b1 and the c2-pawn to c3. What difference does this make?

Summary

In the ending your forces are much reduced, but you still have the same area of territory to cover.

You are much less likely to have a mating attack against the king in the endgame than in the middlegame.

It is so important to think *long-term* in the endgame.

The weaker the pawns, the less active the pieces in the ending.

Chapter Five

Building an Opening Repertoire

- So Many Openings, so Little Time
- Building a Repertoire
- Tricks and Traps
- An Aggressive Attacking Idea
- A Structural Idea

In the earlier chapters of this book, we looked at the general principles of the opening, the middlegame and the ending. Before we can try out our skills in an actual game, there is one practical problem which still has to be answered: What openings do I want to play?

So Many Openings, so Little Time!

The *last* question that will ever be solved in chess is: Which is the best first move for White? Once this is known, then all the secrets of chess will have been discovered! There is no single best move for White (or Black) from the starting position. There are however *better and worse moves*. 1 d4, 1 e4, 1 Nf3, and 1 c4 are the four most common and best opening moves because they all exert some central control right from the first move. By contrast, a move like 1 h4? has absolutely no point and is just a waste of a move.

But what happens after the first move? After 1 e4 for example, Black can play 1...c5 (the Sicilian Defence), 1...e6 (the French Defence) or even 1...g6 (the Modern Defence) to name but a few. Chess seems so daunting if you need to memorise lines against all of them. Don't panic! I'm going to explain how grandmasters build their opening repertories.

Building a Repertoire

The most important factor in dealing with the opening is:

Never forget the General Principles

It is easy to lose sight of the basic principles when the position gets complicated, but these rules – control of the centre, rapid development, king safety and the initiative – are your guidelines in the opening, just as they are guidelines for grandmasters and World Champions. At the very least, *they can help you to reject moves and to narrow down the often confusing range of choices to a manageable number of sensible ones. It is much easier to work out what **is** good once you understand what **isn't** any good.* So as Black, for example, after 1 e4, you don't want to play 1...a5? because it does nothing either for your central control or for your development. That's already one less move to worry about!

It all starts with a Thought

Nobody knows everything and nobody can remember everything. In chess, there is a huge amount that even grandmasters and World Champions don't know. They are always working, always hungry to know more... but it just isn't possible to be perfect!

One thing that distinguishes strong players from the crowd is the fact that they *really know the sort of things they like*. What do I mean by that?

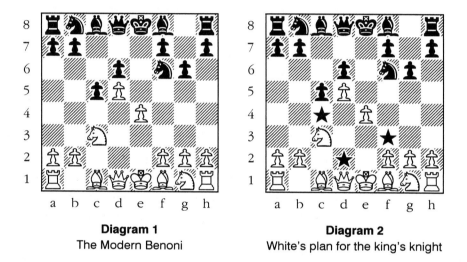

Diagram 1
The Modern Benoni

Diagram 2
White's plan for the king's knight

The position in diagram 1 arises from an opening called the Modern Benoni. The opening moves were

1 d4 Nf6 2 c4 c5 3 d5 e6 4 Nc3 exd5 5 cxd5 d6 6 e4 g6 (see diagram 1)

If you showed a strong player this position, he would *never* say 'Ah, I know 20 complex variations that come from this position.' A strong player would concentrate on his *general aims*: 'Whenever I get this type of position, I always try to transfer my king's knight to c4 via f3 and d2 (see diagram 2).

'From there the knight attacks the d6-pawn which is very weak because Black cannot protect it with any of his other pawns.'

The strong player doesn't *need* to memorise a huge number of variations – he just knows that on one move he will play Nf3, and a few moves later he will play Nd2 and then Nc4. *He knows what he is aiming for generally.*

Strong players are *not* just people who have good recall of the variations recommended by specialist books. They develop their openings around *good general ideas.* The long variations only come about after a great deal of testing, and you should try to follow the same process.

 TIP: An understanding of the general ideas behind the openings is much more important than memorising variations

I know this sounds strange, but hopefully the following examples will make things clearer. What ideas can you base your opening repertoire around? There are three general categories:

1. Tricks and traps
2. An aggressive attacking idea
3. A structural idea

Tricks and Traps

When I think back over the openings that I played when I was seven years old and just starting out, I find that I have forgotten most of them, except for a couple that seem as fresh as if I still played them today. The reason is that these were the ones to which I brought something of myself to them – I had an idea! For example, here was my black opening against 1 e4:

1 e4 e5 2 Nf3 Nf6

This is the Petroff Defence. White's second move attacked the black pawn on e5. Instead of defending the pawn on e5, Black counters with an attack on his opponent's e4-pawn. The fun in playing this opening came from knowing two tricks. One I had to avoid, the other I could set my opponent!

Trick No.1

3 Nxe5 (see diagram 3) Now 3...Nxe4? is a terrible mistake as 4 Qe2! Nf6 5 Nc6+! The knight has discovered a check on the black king by the white queen. However, I knew that **3...d6!** first was the best way for Black as after **4 Nf3 Nxe4 5 Qe2** achieves nothing now due to 5...Qe7! 6 d3 Nf6 with a perfectly good position for Black. Instead **5 d4 d5** (see diagram 4) is normal, but I was happy to play this position as Black.

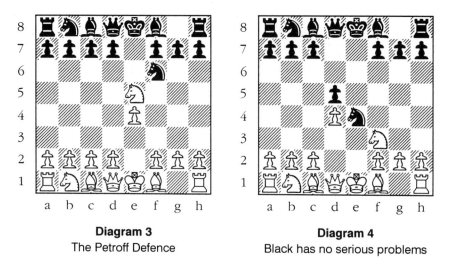

Diagram 3
The Petroff Defence

Diagram 4
Black has no serious problems

Trick No.2

3 Nc3 protecting the threatened central pawn on e4. This is a rare move at grandmaster level, but as a junior I played against it a lot. After **3...Nc6 4 Bc4** was played against me most of the time. All of White's moves have been good central moves, but there is something specific that makes White's last move an inferior choice: a trick that a friend showed me!
4...Nxe4! (see diagram 5) This always came as a shock to my opponents, who at first thought that I had blundered a piece! There are two variations:

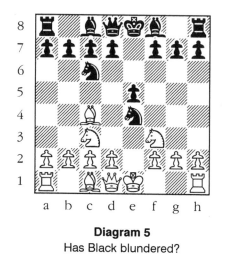

Diagram 5
Has Black blundered?

Diagram 6
Black has a good game

1. **5 Nxe4 d5!**

Black regains the piece he sacrificed temporarily by forking White's knight and bishop. There it is: the trick! Nothing dramatic, it doesn't win on the spot, but it does give Black a very nice position. This idea was at the heart of my black opening repertoire and I built my openings around it. I won a great many games from this position. For example, J. Fletcher-Sadler, British U-11 Championship 1984, continued

6 Bd3 dxe4 7 Bxe4 f6

defending the pawn on e5. White was threatening 8 Bxc6+ bxc6 9 Nxe5.

8 c3

8 Bxc6+ bxc6 would be nasty for Black's pawn structure, but I felt that the two bishops would be adequate compensation.

8...Be6 9 Qe2 Qd7 10 0-0 0-0-0 11 Rd1 Bd5 12 Bxd5 Qxd5 13 b4 Qd3 14 Qxd3 Rxd3 (see diagram 6)

with a good game for Black.

2. **5 Bxf7+ Kxf7 6 Nxe4**

White knew that he would lose back the piece after 5 Nxe4 d5 and so decided to give back the piece only after forcing the black king to move. This is fine in theory; however, there is a very large problem. By losing his pawn on e4, White has lost his foothold in the centre. Just look back to our first chapter and the example of the pawns against the knights – there is only one logical move for Black now!

6...d5! (see diagram 7) **7 Nfg5+**

A desperate attack from White, but 7 Ng3 e4! is also very uncomfortable for him.

7...Ke8! 8 Qf3

Threatening mate on f7 but...

8...Qe7! (see diagram 8)

Black deals with the mate threat and there is still the threat to capture the knight on e4. But when the knight on e4 moves...

9 Nc3 Qxg5!

wins a piece for Black.

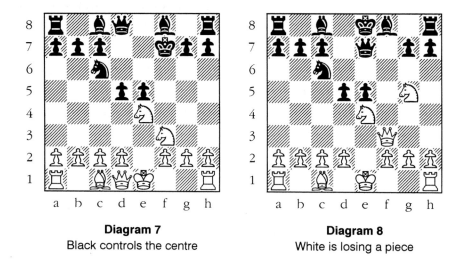

Diagram 7
Black controls the centre

Diagram 8
White is losing a piece

So I became a 1 e4 e5 player as Black because I knew a couple of traps; I had something fresh of my own. This is how all my best openings have come about: I started just with a thought 'Oh, can't I do that?' and then built the rest around it.

An Aggressive Attacking Idea

The next type of idea became the heart of my white opening repertoire when I was 10 and 11. The idea stems from a basic attacking set-up (see diagram 9). In this position, White plays

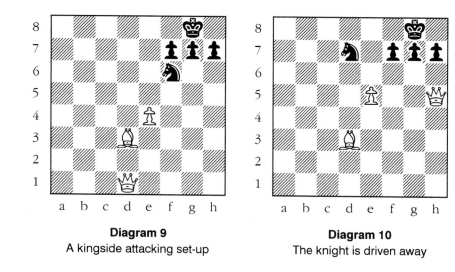

Diagram 9
A kingside attacking set-up

Diagram 10
The knight is driven away

1 e5! This has two points:

1. The bishop on d3 is no longer blocked by the pawn on e4, and now attacks the pawn on h7 which is just next to the black king.

2. From e5, the pawn attacks Black's knight on f6. This is Black's main defensive piece and performs two functions, both helping to defend the pawn on h7 and covering the h5- and g4-squares on the kingside.

The latter point is important because once the knight moves... **1...Nd7** White can bring his queen into the attack with **2 Qh5!** (see diagram 10), attacking h7 in combination with the bishop on d3 and threatening Qxh7 checkmate. Here we see here an idea that was mentioned in Chapter 1 – *the pawns clearing the way for the pieces.*

This idea to launch an attack can be used in a variety of positions. It was shown to me via the London System and helped me in fact to beat my first player rated over 200 BCF (2200 FIDE)! Here is the nicest game that I played with it.

□ Sadler ■ K.Ellis
King's Head Quickplay 1986
London System

---

1 d4 Nf6 2 Nf3 d5 3 Bf4 e6 4 e3 Be7 5 Nbd2 0-0 6 Bd3 Nbd7 7 c3 c5 (see diagram 11)

and now...

8 Ne5! Nxe5 9 dxe5!

This was the idea. At the cost of doubling his pawns, White achieves the desired attacking structure!

9...Nd7 10 Qh5! (see diagram 12)

The white queen comes into the fray, threatening Qxh7+ checkmate. After

10...f5

blocking the threat of mate, I continued with

11 g4!

to open lines against the king. We shall see the rest of this game later in this book.

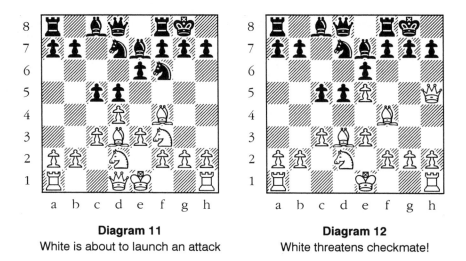

Diagram 11
White is about to launch an attack

Diagram 12
White threatens checkmate!

Here one mechanism formed the basis of my white opening repertoire. Of course, I didn't get this in every game, but it was my 'bread and butter' position – the one I was looking for from the opening.

A Structural Idea

This is similar to the previous idea, but it is purely positional with no definite attacking ideas in mind. You aim simply to establish a certain type of pawn structure that you like and with which you feel comfortable, and then let the opponent deal with it as best he can. Recently as White, I have been experimenting with an idea that I dabbled with as a 10-year-old. It occurs in the English Opening: **1 c4 e5 2 Nc3 Nf6 3 Nf3 Nc6** All the moves so far have been very sound and central. Now White plays an unusual idea: **4 e4** (see diagram 13).

What is this? Didn't I say that this kind of thing was bad? What is White's compensation for the hole that he concedes on d4? You can compare White's pawns on c4 and e4 to two huge pillars that hold everything in place and keep the centre stable. One of Black's ideas was to play ...d7-d5 to open lines for his queenside to develop while gaining central space. After White plays 4 e4, Black no longer has such a possibility. By reducing the opponent's possibilities, White aims to stifle him and to take a grip on the position.

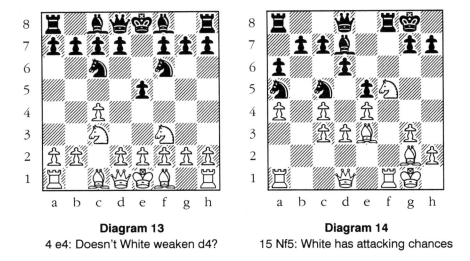

Diagram 13
4 e4: Doesn't White weaken d4?

Diagram 14
15 Nf5: White has attacking chances

White's aim is to play d2-d3, g2-g3, Bg2, 0-0 and then to expand on the kingside with Nh4 and f2-f4. For example, the game Deng Kong Liang-Wolff, US Masters 1998, continued

4...Bb4

Threatening 5...Bxc3 followed by 6...Nxe4.

5 d3 Bxc3+ 6 bxc3 d6 7 g3 0-0 8 Bg2 a6 9 a4 Nd7 10 0-0 Nc5 11 Nh4 Na5 12 Be3 Bd7 13 f4 f6 14 fxe5 fxe5 15 Nf5 (see diagram 14)

with good attacking chances for White.

So the basic principle of opening play is to avoid the memorisation of long variations in favour of carrying out a series of general ideas, based on sound general principles. But how do you find these ideas? Well I hope that this book will stimulate you to think on your own!

Summary

General principles help you to reject moves and to narrow down the often confusing range of choices to a manageable number of sensible ones.

It is much easier to work out what *is* good once you understand what *isn't* any good.

Strong players are distinguished from the crowd by the fact that they really know the sort of things they like.

Strong players develop their openings around *good general ideas*, not long chains of variations.

has placed his light-squared bishop on the long h1-a8 diagonal which was opened when he played 3...dxc4.

As you can see, these are much more aggressive and complicated lines than 3 Bf4. I would recommend that 3 Bf4 is more the type of move you should be playing at the start of your chess career – set up a safe position and then play from it; 3 c4 needs a little more experience.

However, the typical idea of putting pressure on Black's centre and forcing a concession is well worth remembering as it can occur in all kinds of positions. Let's return to 3 Bf4.

3...e6

What do you think of this move? It's a natural move to develop the dark-squared bishop and castle the black king to safety. However, as White is putting no pressure on the black centre, Black could well have taken the opportunity to develop his light-squared bishop outside the pawn chain with 3...Bf5 before developing his kingside. Alternatively, Black could try 3...c5 taking the chance to attack the white centre since White has omitted to do the same to Black's. *Be kind to your pieces!* The move played in the game needlessly makes the light-squared bishop a little passive.

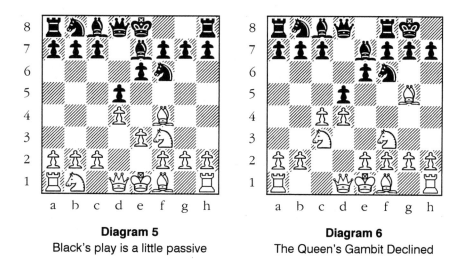

Diagram 5
Black's play is a little passive

Diagram 6
The Queen's Gambit Declined

4 e3 Be7?! (see diagram 5)

Again this is a perfectly decent move, so why am I questioning it a little? I'm going to try to answer something that people are often confused by in chess – they say 'All my moves were natural and normal, just as the books say, so why did I get a difficult position?'

The Balance of the Game

I keep emphasising that chess is a game of balance. For example, in the opening phase I said that you can't have everything you want at once: you often have to offer small things to your opponent in order to get what you want from him.

There is another type of balance in chess – the way the game feels: who is on top, who isn't, who should be attacking, who should be defending.

In the opening, the normal balance of the play is that White probes and Black has to be slightly careful.

So for example, after **3 c4** White attacks the black centre and Black must play carefully as we saw earlier, perhaps with **3...e6 4 Nc3 Be7 5 Bg5 0-0** (see diagram 6) which is the Queen's Gambit Declined.

However, in our game White has done nothing to put pressure immediately on Black's position: 3 Bf4 was a good solid developing move, but it does not go immediately for Black's throat! If White attacks in the opening, Black must be careful; *if White doesn't attack, then... Black can be less careful and look a little more towards what he wants to do!* As we shall see, in our game Black plays exactly the same developing moves against the London System as in the Queen's Gambit Declined. They are not bad moves, but Black could safely play for more. If he doesn't, then the balance swings back to White again – he will have the first opportunity to start an attack in the middle-game.

So for example, I would prefer 3...Bf5 to 3...e6 (which makes the light-squared bishop a little passive) or instead of 4...Be7 (which doesn't ask any questions of White) I would prefer... well, try exercise 3 at the end of this chapter.

At some stage in the game Black will have to make some decisions about how he is going to make things happen for himself. By favouring very quiet development with 4...Be7, Black delays the decision. This is not bad, but Black must realise that by doing this, he is not putting all his problems behind him. He *will* have to answer some questions later all the same. You always have to do some hard work in chess!

5 Nd2 0-0 6 Bd3 Nbd7 (see diagram 7)

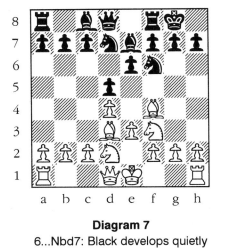

Diagram 7	Diagram 8
6...Nbd7: Black develops quietly	6...0-0: Central pressure from Black

Another slightly strange move. Black's obvious plan is to put a little pressure on the white centre with ...c7-c5.

Why do You put pressure on Your Opponent's Centre?

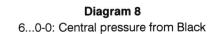

In order to force weaknesses which you can exploit later, you have to be connected with your opponent's position. Putting pressure on the opponent's centre is the first, easy and obvious way to do it. Secondly, by putting pressure on the opponent's centre, you restrict your opponent's choices. The move ...c7-c5 provides a case in point.

After Black's 6...Nd7 move White gains an extra possibility of expanding in the centre with **7 e4** If Black had played 6...c5 (see diagram 8) then after 7 e4 Black would have had the possibility of 7...c4! winning a pawn as 8 Be2 dxe4! 9 Ng5 is met by 9...Qxd4.

This is just an example to show the extra vitality that putting pressure on the opponent's centre gives you and the restraint that it exercises on the opponent. Anyway, back to the game!

7 c3

I just decided to continue with my set-up.

7...c5 (see diagram 9)

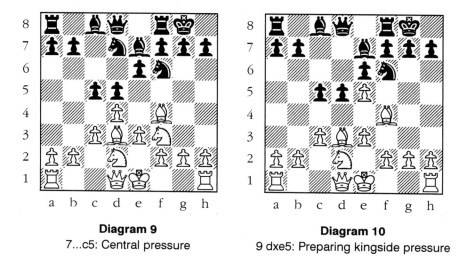

Diagram 9	Diagram 10
7...c5: Central pressure	9 dxe5: Preparing kingside pressure

Now Black finally puts some pressure on the white centre. This is a good decision. Just notice, however, that Black's pieces are not perfectly placed. For example, his knight on d7 would be better on c6, from where it combines with the pawn on c5 against the d4-pawn and leaves d7 free for the light-squared bishop.

By itself, this factor doesn't lead to any sort of disaster. However, the time when you do notice that you've misplaced your pieces, is the time when you have to answer the questions that your opponent is asking you. It's then that you start to think: 'Oh, I wish I'd put that knight on this better square, then I could have done that,' etc.

Even grandmasters can't foresee all the consequences of the moves they play in the opening. They just always try to put their pieces on the most reasonable squares so that when they have to take a decision later, they have as good a version of their position as they can possibly get. The knight is certainly not bad on d7, but unless you have a specific reason for putting it there, the natural move is to put it on c6.

8 Ne5! Nxe5 9 dxe5! (see diagram 10)

And here we are! As we saw in Chapter 5, this is a dangerous attacking set-up. This type of idea is often seen in modern chess: a pawn weakness is accepted in order to gain control of important squares. Take this idea in the Sicilian:

1 e4 c5 2 Nf3 e6 3 d4 cxd4 4 Nxd4 Nc6 This opening is called the Kan Sicilian. **5 Nc3 Qc7 6 Be3 a6 7 Bd3 Nf6 8 0-0 Ne5 9 Nf3** Black's play has been rather strange, I know! However, finally we get to the important position. Here in the game Ponomariov-Salov, Enghien les Bains 1999, Black tried **9...d6 10 Nxe5 dxe5** (see diagram 11).

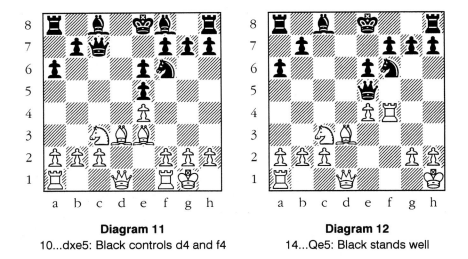

Diagram 11	Diagram 12
10...dxe5: Black controls d4 and f4	14...Qe5: Black stands well

What compensation does Black get for his doubled pawns? Black gains control of the central dark squares on d4 and f4 over which he previously had no influence. White thus can no longer use these squares for himself and they now become outposts for Black's pieces. White is also prevented from gaining space on the kingside with f2-f4. If White plays now **11 f4** then after **11...Bc5! 12 Bxc5 Qxc5+ 13 Kh1 exf4 14 Rxf4 Qe5** (see diagram 12) Black has an excellent position: White has an isolated pawn on e4 and no compensation for it.

 It is sometimes worthwhile accepting pawn weaknesses if you can gain compensating factors elsewhere.

The drawback of this strategy is structural, of course. White has three pawns to Black's two on the queenside whereas Black only has four and a bit to White's four on the kingside! All Black's problems will arise in the ending (see diagram 13).

In this position, only White can create a passed pawn (with c2-

c4, b2-b4, c4-c5, a2-a4, b4-b5 and c5-c6). With his doubled pawn, Black cannot do anything with his own pawns. That is the risk that Black takes: the endings are likely to be bad for him if he gets nothing special from the middlegame. However, Black reckons that his short-term activity and control over the centre *will* give him what he needs.

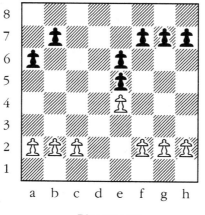

Diagram 13
Black has problems in the endgame

In the main game 9 dxe5 uses this idea for attacking purposes. The other important point is that White's attack comes *with tempo*. 9 dxe5 attacks the black knight on f6, forcing it to move away to avoid capture. That isn't a positive move by Black, it's just something that he has to do. And then White gets the chance straightaway to do something positive himself on the very next move. This attack with gain of tempo is a way for White to force the pace, not allowing his opponent time to breathe. Just as Black thinks he has rid himself of one threat and can start planning to do something positive himself, White hits him with something else.

9...Nd7 10 Qh5 (see diagram 14)

Threatening Qxh7+ checkmate. Now White brings his queen into the attack with gain of tempo.

10...f5

Cutting out the mate on h7. If now 11 exf6 then 11...Nxf6! covers the mate on h7. I played a good move here:

11 g4! (see diagram 15)

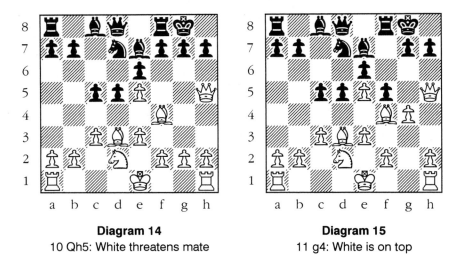

Diagram 14
10 Qh5: White threatens mate

Diagram 15
11 g4: White is on top

We shall cover the rest of the game in the next chapter. First, however, you may be wondering: Why is Black suddenly in trouble? Couldn't he have done something earlier? These are good questions which I'm going to try to answer.

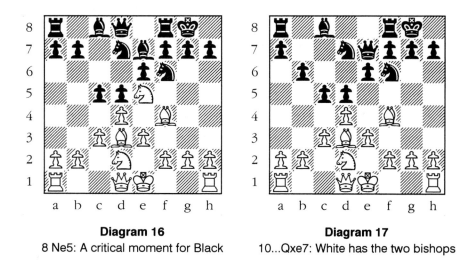

Diagram 16
8 Ne5: A critical moment for Black

Diagram 17
10...Qxe7: White has the two bishops

First of all, the position after 8 Ne5 (see diagram 16) is critical for Black – it is here that he has to solve a number of important problems. Why is this position awkward for Black? Well, let's take a look at some natural moves. If Black tries to develop his light-squared bishop with **8...b6** White can win the bishop pair with **9 Nc6 Qe8 10 Nxe7+ Qxe7** (see diagram 17). Why is this good?

The Two Bishops

The advantage of the bishop pair is an extremely valuable one. When working in combination, the two bishops are a powerful destructive force, able to attack squares of both colours on the same wing. Take the following famous example (see diagram 18):

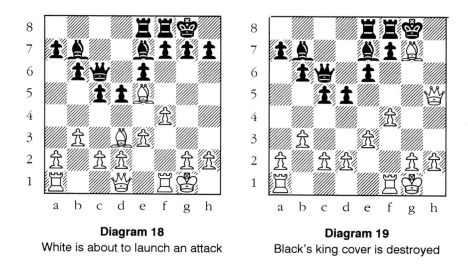

Diagram 18
White is about to launch an attack

Diagram 19
Black's king cover is destroyed

1 Bxh7+! This first sacrifice takes away the light-square cover from the black king. **1...Kxh7 2 Qh5+** White brings in his queen close to the black king with tempo. **2...Kg8 3 Bxg7!!** (see diagram 19) Now White's other bishop rips away the dark-squared pawn cover on the kingside. **3...Kxg7** 3...f6 4 Qg6! is also very painful for Black. **4 Qg4+!** To force the king back to the corner – the area from where it is least likely to escape (unless it jumps off the side of the board!). **4...Kh8 5 Rf3!** The reserves come in. White's threat is Rh3+ and Black can do nothing about it! **5...Rg8 6 Rh3+ Bh4 7 Rxh4 checkmate**

 The ability of the two bishops to attack squares of both colours also makes them very strong at attacking pawn structures.

We can see a good example of this in diagram 20: **1 Bg2 b6 2 Bg3 c5 3 Bb8 a6 4 Ba7 b5 5 Bxc5** winning a pawn. This is very useful in the endgame, when pawns have fewer pieces to defend them and are thus more vulnerable.

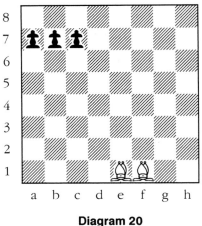

Diagram 20
The bishops working together

Returning to our main game (see diagram 16). Black has put his pieces on slightly passive squares and this restricts his development options somewhat. For example, he cannot try to challenge the knight on e5 with

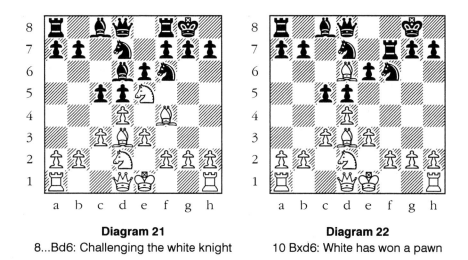

Diagram 21	**Diagram 22**
8...Bd6: Challenging the white knight	10 Bxd6: White has won a pawn

8...Bd6 (see diagram 21) due to **9 Nxf7! Rxf7 10 Bxd6** (see diagram 22) winning a pawn. White's idea is to transfer his queen to the kingside with Qf3-h3 and continue the attack.

But it does seem strange – why is Black's castled king under pressure whereas White's king is safe in the centre?

When you assess a position, you look at the whole position, not

just one factor. Black's king is in its best possible position – it would be much more exposed in the centre. However, as Black's pieces are not putting a great deal of pressure on White, this frees White's pieces to take up more attacking positions than they normally could. White's position is very focused, and directed towards one goal: the black kingside. Black's position is fundamentally sound, but it is hard to point to any one thing that Black is aiming for. It is because of this lack of pressure on his position that White can opt to leave his king a little longer in the centre. But what is the value of this?

Delaying Castling

The general and correct rule is that you should castle as quickly as possible. However, in some circumstances, whilst castling is rarely a bad move, it can perhaps not be the most active move. Quick castling is necessary when there is plenty of pawn action in the centre; the king needs to be on the wing so that it is not caught when the centre is opened. We can thus see why in our game it is possible to leave the king in the centre for a little longer – White is not playing with his pawns to open the centre at all!

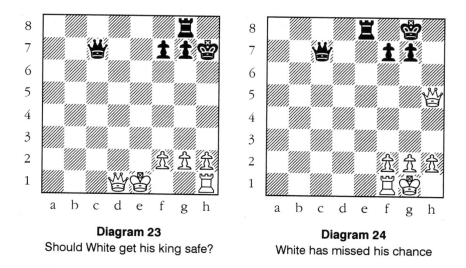

Diagram 23
Should White get his king safe?

Diagram 24
White has missed his chance

But why would you want to delay castling? Take the following example (see diagram 23): What is White's move here? Well the centre is open and White's king is in the centre so... castle kingside? Good general move? Well, yes, but there is something stronger here: **1 Qh5 checkmate!**

Sometimes you spot something that has to be exploited immedi-ately – you have a chance just for one move to go for something; if you wait to consolidate your own position, then the opponent can repair his own position and the chance is gone. For exam-ple, if 1 0-0 then Black plays 1...Re8 and now 2 Qh5+ is met just by 2...Kg8 (see diagram 24). The chance has been missed.

WARNING: Although you can sometimes make a better move than castling, don't forget to get your king safe as soon as possible!

So in our game, White is playing with his king in the centre be-cause first of all the centre is closed and his king is not in any danger, and second because he wants to attack before Black can consolidate. Note though that White is ready to castle at any time if things suddenly get too dangerous.

So what should Black do after move eight? First of all, you have to understand that the balance of the play is swinging White's way. Black has played reasonable but not very chal-lenging moves, and this has given White the chance to move forwards to attack the black position. Black's position is not yet bad, but after another mistake, like 8...Nxe5 as in the game, then things really *will* get difficult! As I said earlier, by not playing active moves earlier (3...e6; 4...Be7) Black delayed the critical moment, when he had to start solving problems, until later. However, he could not get rid of this moment altogether!

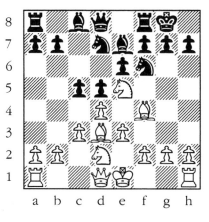

Diagram 25
Black has problems to solve

In diagram 25 Black's problems are:

1. White is about to bring more pieces into play against Black's kingside; and

2. Black's queenside is still not developed.

Of course, the first problem is the most important one – it is no good solving the queenside problem if White is just going to be able to deliver checkmate!

How does Black try and solve this problem? Well, the obvious way is to mobilise more of his pieces to cover the kingside. How can he do this? Well, there is one good way of doing this – he can set up a typical and very solid defensive formation. Consider the following two positions. Which is the most solid?

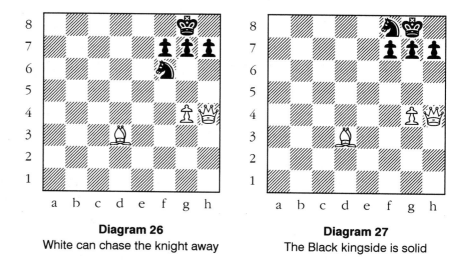

Diagram 26
White can chase the knight away

Diagram 27
The Black kingside is solid

Well, it's diagram 27! In diagram 26, White has the simple move **1 g5!** chasing away the knight from f6, which means that the black knight can no longer defend the h7-pawn against the attack of the bishop on d3 and queen on h4. However, in the second position, the knight is much safer on f8 than f6. In general it's much harder to attack a piece on Black's back rank than one on his third rank. And with defensive pieces, you want them to be safe since they are stopping your king from being checkmated.

This defensive structure of not moving your kingside pawns and putting a knight on f8 to cover h7 is a typical and strong one. The Danish Grandmaster Larsen once said 'With a knight on f8 (or f1 for White) you can never be checkmated!' Not quite true, but...!

So, how do we get this in our game? Let's use the skills we learnt in the knight exercise! To get to f8, a knight has to go via d7. Hmm, we have a knight on d7! And the black rook will have to move from f8. Hmm, there is a free square for the rook on e8! Well, I think the move that we want to play is...

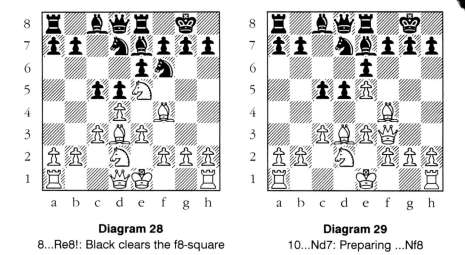

Diagram 28
8...Re8!: Black clears the f8-square

Diagram 29
10...Nd7: Preparing ...Nf8

8...Re8! (see diagram 28) and after **9 Qf3** for example, then Black has two ideas: the immediate 9...Nf8 or my own favourite which is **9...Nxe5 10 dxe5 Nd7** (see diagram 29) when the f6-knight will be transferred to f8! I like this one because, dangerous though the white pawn is on e5, I prefer to get rid of White's strong knight on e5, rather than leave it there. Also, it always helps to exchange pieces when you are defending – the more pieces you can remove from the board, the fewer there are to checkmate you!

In diagram 29, Black has solved his immediate problems: **11 Qh3** is met by **11...Nf8** when nothing too terrible is happening immediately to Black. By bringing his knight back to f8, Black avoided weakening his kingside by moving one of the pawns there. This perhaps explains why in the game after 9...Nd7 White delayed castling and played 10 Qh5! If White played slowly with 10 0-0, for example, then after 10...Re8 11 Qh5 Black is ready to defend with 11...Nf8.

Try it Yourself

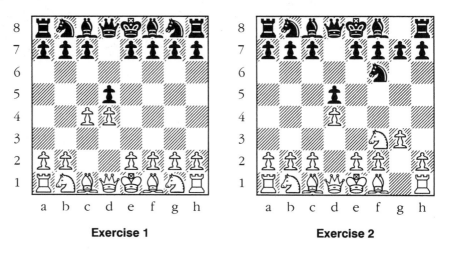

Exercise 1   Exercise 2

Exercise 1: 1 d4 d5 2 c4 What is the point of 2 c4?

Exercise 2: 1 d4 d5 2 Nf3 Nf6 3 g3 Find me a good Black developing move!

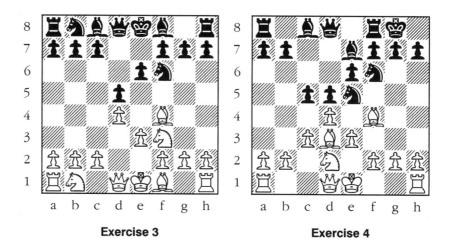

Exercise 3   Exercise 4

Exercise 3: 1 d4 d5 2 Nf3 Nf6 3 Bf4 e6 4 e3 Find a move for Black that challenges the white position!

Exercise 4: Explain the point of 9 dxe5.

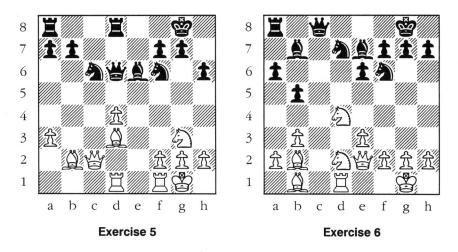

Exercise 5   **Exercise 6**

Exercise 5: This is a position from Sadler-Wilder, Watson, Farley & Williams, London 1989. White has the two bishops, and they are pointing at the black king. Activate them!

Exercise 6: This is a position from San Segundo-Sadler, European Team Championship, Pula 1997. White played **17 e4** with future ideas of e4-e5 and a kingside attack. Find a solid defensive move for Black!

Summary

Place as many of your pieces on active squares as possible.

Good black moves are always slightly different from good white moves, because in the opening Black has to respond to what White is doing.

White always has the chance to strike at Black's position first, so Black is always going to be slightly on the defensive.

By putting pressure on the opponent's centre, you restrict your opponent's choices.

Sometimes you spot something that has to be exploited immediately – you have a chance just for one move to go for something.

Chapter Seven

The Middlegame: Attacking Play

- ■ **Opening Lines for the Pieces**
- ■ **Creating Weaknesses**
- ■ **Using the Queen to attack**

We left the game Sadler-K.Ellis in our last chapter poised at the position in diagram 1.

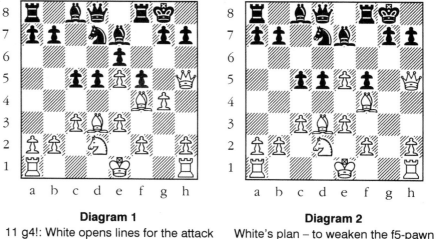

Diagram 1	**Diagram 2**
11 g4!: White opens lines for the attack	White's plan – to weaken the f5-pawn

What was the point of that 11 g4! move?

Although the final part of the attack is often the most spectacular, with pieces being sacrificed everywhere, the most skilful part is always... getting the pieces there in the first place!

There are two important aims to bear in mind while pursuing an attack:

1. To open lines for one's pieces
2. To weaken the opponent's structure and defences

Opening Lines for the Pieces

The ideal attack from our point of view is one in which every single one of our pieces is attacking the king, and none of the opponent's are defending it! This of course rarely happens in practice – your opponents are never *that* helpful – but the general aim is to get as close to this ideal as possible. Why? Because, the more firepower you have, and the less defensive power the opponent has, the more likely you are to succeed with your attack and win the game. It's all about making things simple for yourself! So, you don't just want to attack with your queen and minor pieces, you want to use your rooks as well. You would prefer not to have to sacrifice a rook to get rid of a defending pawn if you can do it with a pawn.

Why do you want to open a file? In order to open a path for your pieces to get to the opponent's position. Your pieces can't do anything if they can't get near to your opponent's structure. How do you open a file for your pieces to use? Well, you have to get rid of your own pawn on that file. So, going back to diagram 1, we see one of the aims of 11 g4!: White wants to open the g-file by exchanging his g-pawn for Black's f-pawn. Why does he want to open this particular file? Well, the black king is on the g-file, with only a pawn covering it, which doesn't make it a particularly tough defensive wall. A rook on that file will definitely make the king very nervous!

Creating Weaknesses

The other aim of 11 g4! is to weaken Black's defences. How is that? Well, Black's pawn on f5 forms a barrier against White's combined attack against the h7-pawn with his bishop on d3 and the queen on h5. It is a very important pawn, and seemingly secure because it is protected by the pawn on e6. But what if that pawn on e6 wasn't there? (see diagram 2)

The f5-pawn would be much weaker – in fact, White would be threatening to take it immediately. With 11 g4! White is aiming to make that exact scenario happen: he intends 12 gxf5 exf5 and... hey presto, he has achieved his aim!

I always think of this type of manoeuvre as 'diluting the opponent's structure'. It is just like adding water to a drink to make it weaker. The pawn on f5 is still where it used to be, but it has been diluted in strength – it has lost half of its support and is suddenly very vulnerable.

So 11 g4! is a very nice multi-purpose attacking move, both opening lines against Black's kingside and 'diluting' Black's defensive pawn structure.

Now we can see why I recommended the defensive manoeuvre of putting the knight on f8, starting with 8...Re8! in preference to Black's idea in the game of 10...f5.

WARNING: By moving pawns in front of your king, you give the opponent targets to attack – the closer they are to his position, the easier they are to reach.

So by playing 10...f5, Black gave his opponent a very easy way to connect with his position: **11 g4!**

Instead of 10...f5, **10...g6** (see diagram 3) would have been a better choice, although after **11 Qg4** White intends to connect with Black's position with h4-h5. The game Sadler-C.Holland, Islington Open 1985, is a good example of the problems Black faces here: **11...f5 12 Qg3 Kg7 13 Nf3 h6 14 h4 Rb8 15 Qh3!** (the right plan, looking for g2-g4 again!) **15...h5 16 Ng5 Bxg5 17 hxg5 b5 18 f3 c4 19 Bc2 Nc5 20 g4!** (see diagram 4) with a dangerous attack for White.

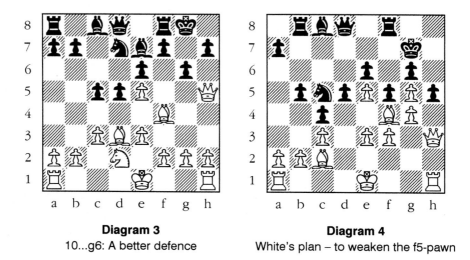

Diagram 3
10...g6: A better defence

Diagram 4
White's plan – to weaken the f5-pawn

Let's return to the main game after 11 g4!

11...Nb6

White's threat was to win a pawn by playing 12 gxf5 exf5 13 Bxf5, so by uncovering the defence of the light-squared bishop on c8 for the pawn on f5, Black prevents this. However, this is a definite concession from Black as he has had to move his knight *away* from the kingside (where all the action is taking place) in order to defend his pawn. What would have happened if Black had played 11...g6 and after 12 Qh6 then 12...fxg4? (see diagram 5) Well, then White has a forced winning combination. Can you see it?

13 Bxg6! hxg6 14 Qxg6+ Kh8 (see diagram 6). White desperately wants to clear the g4-pawn from the g-file in order to check the black king with Rg1+. How does White do this? Well, he use a series of checks: 15 Qh5+! Kg8 16 Qxg4+! (clearing the

Qxg6+ and White has a completely winning position.

I hope that this has given you some helpful ideas on general attacking play. The reason that good players often make attacking look easy is because they use *all* the weapons at their disposal – they use their pawns to soften up the opponent, and then put *everything* towards the opponent's king; not just a few pieces, *everything*... down to the last rook!

Summary

There are two important aims to bear in mind while pursuing an attack: to open lines for one's pieces and to weaken the opponent's structure and defences.

The queen is the 'finishing off' piece. The piece that, once you've sacrificed plenty of 'little guys' to break open the position, mops up the mess and applies the finishing touches.

Good players make attacking look easy because they use *all* the weapons at their disposal.

Chapter Eight

The Middlegame: Positional Play

- Assessing a Position
- Knowing when to attack
- The Dangers of Materialism
- Regrouping the Pieces

In this chapter, we shall examine the positional, manoeuvring side of the game. We join our game after Black's 16th move. And would you believe it... it's one of mine again!

Assessing a Position

The situation in diagram 1 (below) is quite complicated, with many different factors, so we will spend some time on it.

□ Richardson ■ Sadler
Islington Open 1995

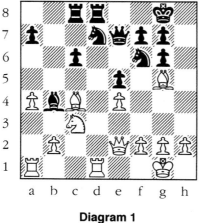

Diagram 1
Does Black have pawn weaknesses?

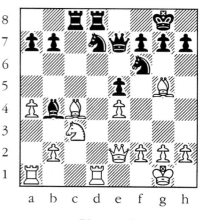

Diagram 2
'Mending' the black pawns

 TIP: Whenever you come across a new position, you have to just stop for a moment and assess it, to find out who is better and why!

In terms of pawn weaknesses, White is definitely superior: Black has doubled pawns on the kingside and two isolated pawns on the queenside on c6 and a7. White also has the two bishops, so... the position is clearly better for him? It's not that simple!

White also has his weaknesses and they are all to do with squares. Just look for a moment at Black's pawn weaknesses – the doubled pawn on g6 and the isolated pawn on c6. Though they are static weaknesses, they do perform a vital dynamic function. The white central pawn on e4 gives the white pieces (particularly a white knight) outposts on f5 and d5. Now if you were to imagine a 'repaired' black structure with the g6-pawn on h7 and the c6-pawn on b7 (see diagram 2) then White to move would have the very annoying **17 Nd5** forking Black's queen and bishop; the knight cannot be taken because the knight on f6 is pinned to the queen on e7 by White's bishop on g5. However, with Black's 'damaged' structure, White's knight has precious few prospects – the g6-pawn controls the f5-square, and even more crucially, the pawn on c6 controls the d5-square. We saw this same idea in Chapter 6 with Salov's idea of taking on doubled e-pawns to reduce the options of his opponent's pieces.

What are Black's strengths in this position? Well, let's apply the same test to White that we have just applied to Black. Black has a central pawn on e5 that gives two nice knight outposts on f4 and d4, but... well, there are no buts actually! This is it – White's nice neat structure means that Black is actually free to try to put a knight on f4, or most temptingly of all, on d4. Okay, time for testing your knight manoeuvring skills! Get a knight to d4 *via the most active route.* Can you see it?

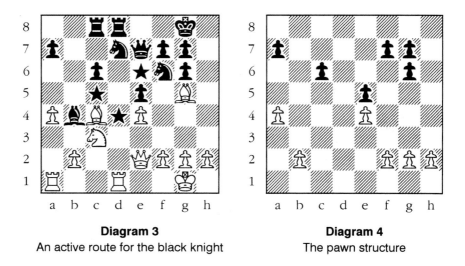

Diagram 3
An active route for the black knight

Diagram 4
The pawn structure

It's c7-e6-d4. Why is this the most active route? Two reasons:

1. From c5, the knight combines against the e4-pawn with the knight on f6 and the bishop on b4 (which can remove one of the defenders of e4 with ...Bxc3). Thus the threat of winning White's e-pawn will always be 'in the air'.

2. From c5, the knight attacks White's other weakness.

What is White's other weakness? Well, let's take all the pieces off, and just look at the pawns – this should make it clearer (see diagram 4). We already know the full horror of Black's queenside structure, but let's take a look at White's. It is not ideal. The pawn on b2 is on a half-open file – if you imagine a black rook on b8 you can see how easy it is to attack. Now if the white a-pawn were on a2, there would be no problem – White could simply play b2-b3 and his pawn would be protected, but here... well, the pawn is very vulnerable. There are a number of tempting squares for Black's major pieces on the queenside as well – how about a queen on b3 attacking both pawns, or a rook on b4 with the same result? Very tasty! In other words, though White's queenside structure is 'cleaner' than Black's, it is potentially just as weak, simply because there are so many tempting squares for Black's pieces to aim for. From c5 for example, the black knight attacks both the b3-square and the pawn on a4.

TIP: A 'visually' attractive pawn structure is not necessarily as good as it appears. Take a close look at any weak squares in it and how they might be exploited.

Of course, at the moment White's light-squared bishop on c4 is covering b3. However, the question arises – what is White going to do about Black's main plan of putting a knight on d4? White doesn't really want to allow it to come there, so perhaps it is worth giving up the bishop on c4 by capturing the knight when it comes to e6? This is probably necessary, but then... your queenside light squares suddenly lack the protection that the light-squared bishop was giving them!

As you can see, so many things are connected in chess – there are consequences to everything that you do. The only reason that Black's position is not bad is because of this combination of the plan to transfer the knight to d4 and the potential weakness of White's queenside pawns on a4 and b2. Put the white pawn back on the more secure a2-square and White is a little better because he has fewer worries about his queenside.

White's plan now should have been just to consolidate his position, starting perhaps with 17 f3 in order to cement the e-pawn. The position is equal, but there are chances for both sides.

Knowing when to attack

However, White decided that due to Black's kingside pawn weaknesses, he had a chance of a kingside attack and played

17 Rd3? Nc5

Starting Black's plan.

18 Rh3? Ne6 (see diagram 5)

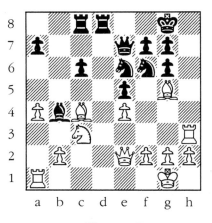

Diagram 5
18...Ne6: White tries a kingside attack

So what attracted White to the idea of a kingside attack? It was mainly the fact that due to his doubled g-pawns, Black has no pawn barrier on the h-file. White felt that this gave him a good opportunity to mate Black down the h-file.

 WARNING: Although it is very tempting to launch an attack, it is not always a good idea.

The attack in Chapters 6 and 7 worked because White was able to work up a huge advantage in the number of pieces he had mobilised. By attacking Black with gain of tempo, by creating threats that always had to be answered, White managed to bring his pieces into the action with the minimum of delay. Here, however, Black is already fully developed and White is going to need a great deal of time to get his pieces into the right positions: two moves already to bring the rook to h3, and three more to bring the white queen to h4 and threaten mate (Qg3-h4). If Black, from an already active, fully developed position, cannot deal with this one threat in five moves, it would be absolutely amazing! Already Black is interfering with White's plans – his last move prepares to play the knight to d4 and attacks the bishop on g5 en route. If 19 Bxf6 Qxf6 then the situation is even worse for White: the black queen on f6 now controls the h4-square – even if White manages to get his queen to the h-file, Black can now just exchange it.

Here White made a good practical decision. He realised that he had misplaced his pieces badly and wasted time on a plan that would not work. Instead of just trying to pursue it, and misplacing the rest of his army in the process, he swallowed his pride and brought his pieces back to try and repair the damage. If you can save a draw by hanging in there, it's much better than losing a game by throwing all your pieces into something that you know won't work. We all make mistakes, but it's the people who are prepared to work hard to repair and correct their errors who succeed in the end.

19 Bxe6 Qxe6 (see diagram 6)

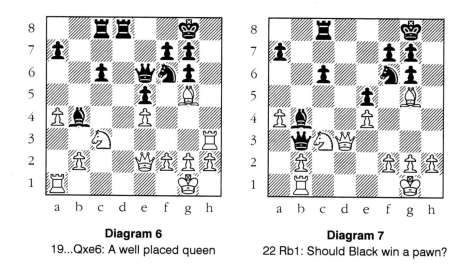

Diagram 6
19...Qxe6: A well placed queen

Diagram 7
22 Rb1: Should Black win a pawn?

From e6, the queen aims for the weak queenside light squares.

20 Rd3

The rook has no purpose on h3 if White cannot attack. For that reason, White exchanges it, while at the same time trying to counter Black's present control of the d-file.

20...Rxd3 21 Qxd3 Qb3

A great square for the queen!

22 Rb1 (see diagram 7)

The Dangers of Materialism

Now we come to a very interesting point in the game. *The biggest problem of playing a better position is knowing when to cash in your advantage.* You may be able to win a pawn for example, but at the cost of freeing the opponent's position; or you could just continue to keep the opponent in a bind, but give up the chance to win a pawn...

This same dilemma came up in the previous chapter – at some stage, I could have played Bh6 to win the exchange, but I decided instead to keep going on with my attack. The risk of course is that by spurning an opportunity now to win something... you may never get another chance.

Here, I spent a long time pondering whether to win a pawn with 22...Bxc3 23 bxc3 Qxa4 (see diagram 8).

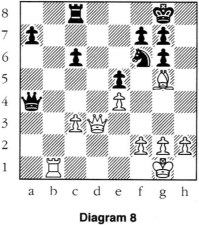

Diagram 8
Black is a pawn up

There is absolutely nothing wrong tactically with this move – it wins a pawn fair and square, and I'm attacking White's pawn on e4. But, after 24 f3 defending it quietly, what happens? I started to think what I had gained by this – an extra passed, but quite weak, a-pawn – and compare it with what I'd given up. White's rook used to be passive, defending a pawn on b2, but now look at it, lording it over the open b-file. My queen used to cause White tremendous pain, attacking pawns on a4 and b2, pinning the knight on c3 to the queen on d3 whilst tying down the rook to the defence of b2... but look at it now – offside on a4, with no targets to attack, and no pieces to restrict... I decided that this was more freedom than White deserved.

It takes a great deal of confidence to spurn the opportunity to win something and just to keep the pressure on the opponent, but it is often the very best and even the safest way of playing.

TIP: Keep your opponent tied up, and trust that as you put even more pressure on him, you will eventually gain a bigger reward.

Note also that the pawn on a4 is not running away – you have the feeling that there will always be some new chance to win this pawn at a later stage.

22...Rb8

Threatening to win the knight with 23...Bxc3 as 24 bxc3 Qxb1 wins a rook.

23 Bd2

Forced, to defend against the threat of ...Bxc3.

23...Ba5! (see diagram 9)

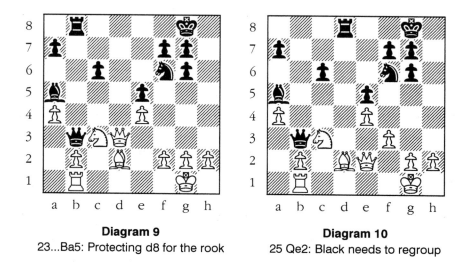

Diagram 9	Diagram 10
23...Ba5: Protecting d8 for the rook	25 Qe2: Black needs to regroup

A nice move that makes connections within Black's position.

By protecting the d8-square one more time, Black secures the move ...Rd8 for his rook, taking control of the d-file and reducing the activity of the white queen. In this way, the black rook can now play both on the b-file and the d-file.

24 f3

White keeps on shoring up his position – with this move, he protects the e4-pawn more securely.

24...Rd8 25 Qe2 (see diagram 10)

Regrouping the Pieces

A critical position has arisen. White has defended very sensibly, bringing his pieces back, and consolidating his position with moves like f2-f3. Black's position looks really good, but how can he improve it? Immediate entries like 25...Qc2 are adequately dealt with by 26 Be3!, aiming for an exchange of queens. But aren't Black's pieces doing all they can possibly do? Well, let's take them one by one:

The queen is doing a marvellous job, attacking the pawns on b2 and a4, tying down the rook to the defence of the b2-pawn, and constantly threatening to enter further into White's position – you can't improve on that!

The rook is also doing well, either on the only open file on the board as here, or attacking the b2-pawn from b8 on the half-open b-file. You can't ask for more!

The bishop is attacking the knight on c3, ever ready to exchange it to remove White's defender of the a-pawn and allow the queen to capture it.

The knight... Hmm, the knight. What is the knight doing in fact? It looks good on f6, but what is it actually attacking? The pawn on e4 is securely defended – it isn't tying the white pieces down to anything. Aha! So this might be a way to put extra pressure on White's position – to bring all of Black's pieces into the action. But how? Well, I tried before to bring a knight to the d4-outpost and it cost White one of his bishops and the defence of his queenside light squares. So... how about trying it again? Knight manoeuvring skills to the ready! How do you get this knight from f6 to d4? There are three ways: ...Nf6-d7-f8-

e6-d4, ...Nf6-d7-c5-e6-d4, ...Nf6-e8-c7-e6-d4. I think all are possible. I preferred...

25...Ne8

...simply because I felt happier not blocking my rook on the d-file for one move by playing 25...Nd7. But it was simply a personal matter of taste: I don't think that there is anything wrong with 25...Nd7.

> **NOTE: Strong players are always trying to involve as many pieces as possible in their attacks.**

26 Be1 Nc7 27 Rc1 Ne6 28 Qc2 (see diagram 11)

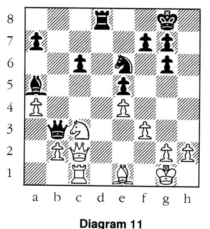

Diagram 11
28 Qc2: Should Black swop queens?

White is doggedly sticking to his defensive task. With this move, he hopes to exchange off queens. Black says...

28...Qb6+!

No! This is a similar situation to the one we encountered in the previous chapter. It's easy to get worried when you have to retreat a piece – you think that you've done something wrong or that your opponent is starting to escape, but it's really important to remain calm. If your advantage entirely depended on your queen being on b3 and you were forced to retreat it, then... you might well be in trouble, but here Black has so much! Well-placed pieces, white queenside weaknesses that are not going away... It's like we said in the previous chapter when White had to play Qh3: fine, *she'll be back!* And remem-

weaknesses – the pawns on a7 and c6 – there is a big difference: White's pawns are much easier to attack. Whereas nothing is attacking Black's pawns, the black queen is attacking the a4-pawn, the black rook is attacking the e4-pawn and Black is ready to destroy one of the key defenders of both pawns by playing ...Bxc3. Something has to drop.

35 Rd1 Bxc3 36 Bxc3 Ne2! (see diagram 19)

Something is definitely going to go – the e4- and a4-pawns are hanging and Black is forking the white queen and the white bishop.

37 Qf3

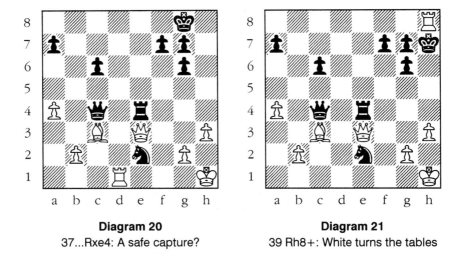

Diagram 20
37...Rxe4: A safe capture?

Diagram 21
39 Rh8+: White turns the tables

You always have to watch out in chess, even when things are going your way. If White had played 37 Qe3 is there anything wrong with 37...Rxe4? (see diagram 20) There certainly is! 38 Rd8+ Kh7 39 Rh8+!! (see diagram 21) Kxh8 40 Qh6+! Aah! 40...Kg8 41 Qxg7+ checkmate.

However, if Black is careful and plays 37...Nxc3 first, then White doesn't get his tactical trick, and the position becomes very similar to the game.

37...Rxe4

Pawn up!

38 a5

The pawn was attacked so White moves it to a protected square.

38...a6

A nice quiet move – the pawn is protected by the queen here. Black is saying to White 'What can you do?' 39 Rd8+ looks tempting but after 39...Kh7 White has no follow-up.

39 Qd3

White decides that since the middlegame is bad for him, he should look for salvation in the endgame.

39...Nxc3 40 Qxc4 Rxc4 41 bxc3

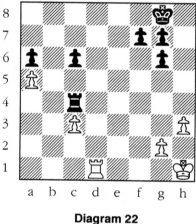

Diagram 22
Black is a pawn up in the endgame

and the ending which we shall look at in Chapter 9 has arisen (see diagram 22). I hope you have developed some idea in the last two chapters about how each player tries to implement general principles in the middlegame. In particular, strong players are always trying to involve as many pieces as possible in their attacks – we saw it in the first game, and we saw it here with 25...Ne8 for example.

Try it Yourself

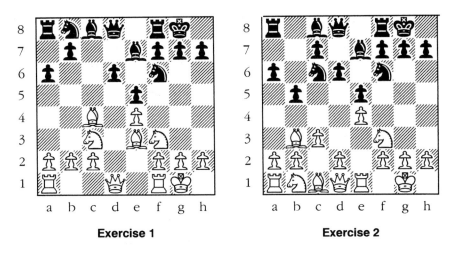

Exercise 1   Exercise 2

Exercise 1: Assess the weaknesses in Black's structure and suggest a way in which they might 'repaired'.

Exercise 2: Assess Black's structural weakness and 'repair' it.

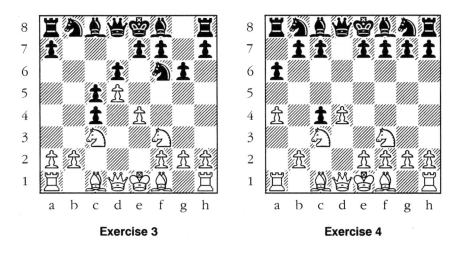

Exercise 3   Exercise 4

Exercise 3: Sadler-Adams, Crewe 1993. White is a pawn down, but he could simply recapture it with 7 Bxc4. However, he has a better move. *How can White disrupt Black's position and worsen his structure?*

Exercise 4: Auchenberg-Sadler, Copenhagen 1992. Find White's weakness, and get your knight aiming towards it!

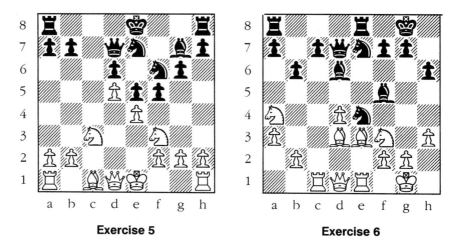

Exercise 5   **Exercise 6**

Exercise 5: Sadler-Dorfman, Cannes 1996. Find Black's weak square and put a knight there!

Exercise 6: Hauchard-Sadler, Cannes 1996. White played **17 Ne5 Bxe5 18 dxe5**. Is there anything wrong with this?

Summary

Whenever you come to a new position, you have to just stop for a moment and assess it, to find out *who is better and why*!

The biggest problem of playing a better position is knowing when to cash in your advantage.

Keep your opponent tied up, and trust that as you put even more pressure on him, you will eventually gain a bigger reward.

If you are in a superior position and there is one tactical motif present – like a fork of the king and rook – then look very carefully, be prepared to put in some effort as you can often find a shortcut to victory.

You shouldn't rush at all. Give your opponent the chance to make a mistake.

Chapter Nine

Endgame Play

- Staying Calm!
- Forming a Plan
- Using the King
- Finishing off

In the previous chapter, we reached this position (see diagram 1).

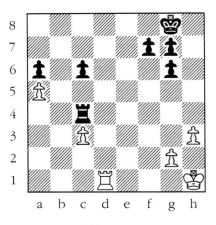

Diagram 1
Black is a pawn up in the endgame

Staying Calm!

The most important thing when you reach an endgame in a practical game is to *take a few minutes to try and get yourself into a calm frame of mind.* The middlegame is always an exciting time of the game – you worry about missing moves, pieces fly all over the board, you get excited or depressed – but you need a completely different attitude to play endings well. You need to be thinking about long-term plans, not feverishly calculating variations or trying to attack the opponent's king. I always just fetch a drink and something to eat, just to force myself to take a little longer than I would normally.

It can often seem unfair as well that after playing so well, you have 'only' reached an ending with an extra pawn. Why after playing so many good moves do you still have extra work to do? I know the feeling, but sometimes when you come up against a tough opponent, you have to put a lot of work in!

NOTE: If you are a pawn up in the ending, you should be enjoying the position a lot more than your opponent.

Being material up should be **fun!** *Having a good position should be* **fun!** So although you may have to work hard, just remember that life on your side of the board is much better than life on your opponent's side. If you don't believe me, walk round to the other side of the board to have a look. You'll soon come running back to your side!

In diagram 1 Black is a pawn up and his pieces are well placed, so it's clear that White can only hope for a draw at best.

The crucial area of the position is the queenside. Why is this? Well, imagine that all the queenside pawns have been exchanged (see diagram 2):

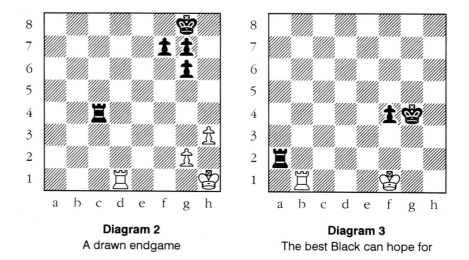

Diagram 2
A drawn endgame

Diagram 3
The best Black can hope for

This position is a draw. Why? Because in order to win an endgame, Black has to queen a pawn, and in order to queen a pawn Black has to create a passed pawn. The only place Black can create a passed pawn is on the kingside... right in front of White's king which is ideally placed to blockade it.

TIP: You always want to create passed pawns far away from the opponent's king.

The very best that Black can get is something like this (see diagram 3); and even this is not winning. How does White draw this?

In endings of this type, you always have to try to think first what position the opponent is aiming for, and then reason how to stop him. Black wants this position but with his king on g3 and his pawn on f3 because then he is completely winning: **1...Rh2** Threatening ...Rh2 checkmate. **2 Kg1 f2+ 3 Kf1 Rh1+** winning the rook. So going back to the first diagram, we see that Black's next move is clearly going to be ...Kg3. So, White plays

1 Rb3! to stop it. Black replies with **1...f3** Now, if White dallies, Black will play ...Kg3. However, White *now* plays **2 Rb8! Kg3 3 Rg8+ Kf4 4 Rf8+** and checks Black until kingdom come.

Note how White forces the pawn to f3 before trying to check round the back. Had he played **1 Rb8** first, then **1...Kg3! 2 Rg8+ Kf3** would set White big problems. Black always tries to use his pawn to shield his king from checks in this type of ending, so by drawing the pawn forward, White takes away the shield for checks from the back.

Going back to the game, we appreciate that Black has to be very careful that all the queenside pawns do not get exchanged, otherwise the game will just be drawn.

Having got this general principle sorted out, we now look at the specific situation in diagram 1. First of all, can Black win another pawn with **41...Rxc3?** No, because then White plays **42 Rd8+ Kh7 43 Ra8!** and regains the a-pawn. Since White wants to exchange off all the queenside pawns, it is obviously good for him to exchange two of the pawns on that wing. Here this gives him a passed a-pawn to match Black's c-pawn. In fact this position is just drawn as White will push his a-pawn and eventually trade it for Black's c-pawn: **43...c5 44 Rxa6 c4 45 Rc6 Rc1+ 46 Kh2 c3 47 a6 c2 48 a7 Ra1** Forced. **49 Rxc2 Rxa7** with a draw. This manoeuvre of Rd8+-a8xa6 is White's threat in this position.

Forming a Plan

So, now as Black, after this preliminary inspection, we have the following facts clear in our mind:

1. Black is a pawn up and he is the one playing for a win – White can only hope to grovel a draw.

2. White's plan is to swap off all the queenside pawns when the resulting position with rook and three pawns against rook and two pawns all on the same side is known to be a theoretical draw.

3. If White manages to swap off an asymmetrical pair of pawns

(e.g. the a-pawn for his c-pawn or the c-pawn for his a-pawn), then he is likely to be able to force off all the queenside pawns.

4. His threat is to make this happen with Rd8-a8xa6.

What is Black's idea? Simple — if he wants to keep the game alive, he *must* find a way to answer White's rook manoeuvre. Ideally, he could protect his a-pawn when White attacks it with Ra8. Well, once you put it like this, there seems to be a very good square available for the black rook: c5. From c5, the rook threatens both of White's queenside pawns, and the manoeuvre Rd8-a8 can be met by ...Rxa5, not just protecting the a- pawn, but winning a pawn as well! On top of that, Black is threatening to take the a5-pawn immediately. Wow!

41...Rc5! (see diagram 4)

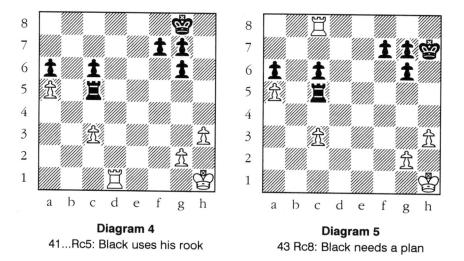

Diagram 4
41...Rc5: Black uses his rook

Diagram 5
43 Rc8: Black needs a plan

How can White hang on? The threat is to take the a5-pawn. White's only hope is to attack the pawn that would be abandoned were Black to take the a-pawn: Black's c-pawn. This is White's only idea that does not allow Black to capture a further pawn immediately.

42 Rd8+ Kh7 43 Rc8 (see diagram 5)

So the first flurry of moves has ended. Black's first concern was to prevent White from swapping off pawns and he has achieved this; now the next stage begins — he can start planning and thinking of something positive to do.

TIP: We have said throughout the book how crucial it is to try to bring all your pieces into the action, and this is especially true in endings – you have so little firepower, you can't afford to waste any!

The black rook is magnificently placed – it attacks two pawns and defends the entire queenside. It also ties down the white rook, which rook cannot abandon its attack of the c6-pawn because otherwise Black will win one of his split pawns. This means that the rook is not free to harass the black pawns. This rook on c5 is a star! However, you do have a piece that isn't working: the king. It's time to bring it into play! Where is it heading? Well, it's heading for weaknesses. Those split pawns on the queenside look mighty tempting!

Using the King

43...g5! 44 Kg1 Kg6 45 Kf2 Kf5 (see diagram 6)

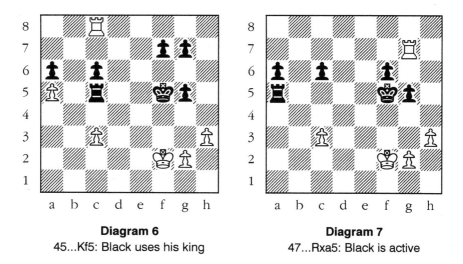

Diagram 6
45...Kf5: Black uses his king

Diagram 7
47...Rxa5: Black is active

It's coming in! Note that White cannot put his king to the third rank with 46 Ke3 because of 46...Rxc3+!, winning the c-pawn with tempo.

46 Rc7 f6

My original intention had been to play 46...Ke6 and then to move my kingside pawns to g6 and f5, away from the attack of the rook on c7, before switching my king to the queenside. However, I started to worry about 47 Ke2 g6 48 Kd3 f5 49 Kd4 when I felt that the white king was becoming too active in comparison to mine. So I opted to allow an exchange of pawns in order to keep my king active.

47 Rxg7 Rxa5 (see diagram 7)

White has swapped off a pair of pawns, but his problems remain. His first concern is to deal with Black's threats which are either 48...Ra2+ 49 Kf3 Ra3 winning the c-pawn, or 48...Rc5 49 Ra7 a5 followed by the advance of the black king. White still cannot move his king to the third rank to block this advance because then the c-pawn will be taken with check. White's biggest problem is that his king is very passive compared to Black's: Black always seems to have ways to improve his position, but White can't really do the same. This explains White's next move:

48 Ke3

White takes the chance to advance his king to the third rank while the black rook is not attacking the c-pawn, but this move has another drawback. I had expected 48 Ra7 attacking the a-pawn and trying to keep the black rook's activity to a minimum. I was planning to respond with 48...Ke4 heading for the c3-pawn – White is lost as Black's king will shepherd his c-pawn home after taking White's pawn.

In the game, the white king heads for Black's queenside pawns. However, in so doing it has to abandon the protection of the kingside pawns. This must be Black's new target – circumstances do change. The support of a piece can mean that a weakness is no longer a weakness. However, in endings there is always a consequence – if you give support to something, you must be withdrawing it from somewhere else – in this case, the kingside. Black's king is already well placed there – it has a clear entry route via f4 into g3. What is needed is to make sure that Black can cover his pawns while his king is away eating White's own pawns. All Black's weak pawns are on the third rank, so a third-rank square for the rook seems the logical choice.

48...Re5+!

Heading for e6.

49 Kd4 Kf4!

Black has forced his way into the kingside – if White is going to do anything, he has to do it now.

50 Ra7 (see diagram 8)

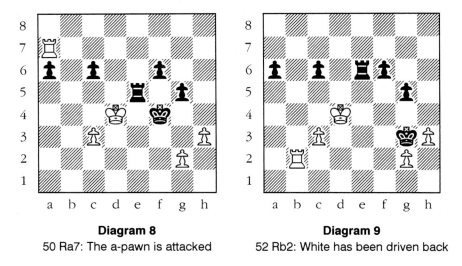

Diagram 8
50 Ra7: The a-pawn is attacked

Diagram 9
52 Rb2: White has been driven back

White is threatening to take the a-pawn. What is the most economical way for Black to defend it?

50...Re6!

A really nice move! White cannot take the a pawn with 51 Rxa6 due to 51...c5+! winning the rook! Meanwhile, Black is threatening to win White's kingside pawns with ...K-g3xg2. White's rook has to return home, but now it is completely passive.

51 Rb7 Kg3 52 Rb2 (see diagram 9)

Finishing off

Right, deep breath! Let's finish off this game! What is White intending first of all? Can he do anything that might be annoying? Well, White might play his king to c5 and b6 attacking Black's queenside pawns and gaining some counterplay. If possible, Black would rather not allow White *any* chances – why should he? How can Black stop this king manoeuvre?

52...Re5!

Taking c5 away from the white king.

53 Ra2 c5+ 54 Kc4 f5 (see diagram 10)

White's king is no longer able to cause trouble by itself now. Only the white rook can capture the black pawns, but if it leaves the second rank, then the g2-pawn goes.

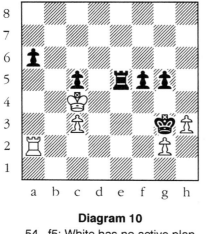

Diagram 10

54...f5: White has no active plan

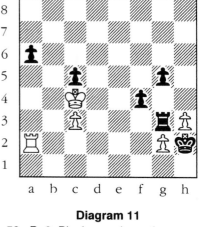

Diagram 11

58...Rg3: Black rounds up the g-pawn

Black has many possible ideas. I was planning to play my pawn to f4 and then capture the g-pawn with my rook. For example, 55 Rb2 f4 56 Ra2 Kh2 57 Rb2 Re3 58 Ra2 Rg3 (see diagram 11) with an easy win. White went for broke, but that didn't work either...

55 Rxa6 Kxg2 56 Rg6 f4 57 h4 f3 58 Rxg5+ Rxg5 59 hxg5 f2 60 Kxc5 f1Q 61 c4 Qf5+ 62 Kd6 Qg6+

And White resigned. This game demonstrates quite nicely the general way of thinking that is necessary to play endings – setting out the problems in a clear way, and then acting on them. Endings always have a different rhythm to middlegames – you have to stop sometimes, give all your attention to holding your position (41...Rc5) and then after that everything feels easy and smooth.

Try it Yourself

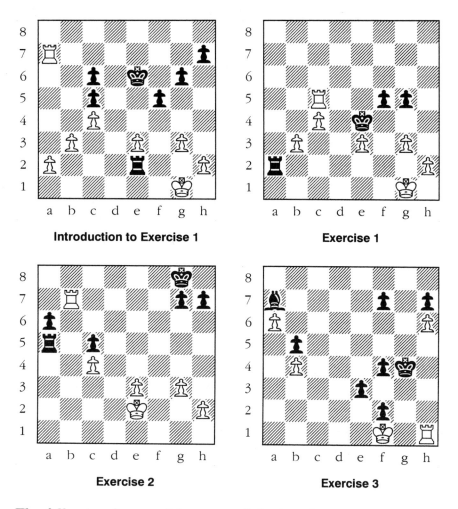

Introduction to Exercise 1

Exercise 1

Exercise 2

Exercise 3

The following four positions are all designed to test a crucial endgame skill: activating the king.

Exercise 1: It is Black to play in the game Lilienthal-Smyslov, match tournament 1941. This was one of the first examples I saw of the power of the active king, and it really made quite an impression on me – I still remember it!

Black is a pawn down and all his pawns are weak. Passive defence is thus doomed to defeat. Black must counterattack, using the poor position of the white king and the activity of the black rook. **1...g5! 2 Rxh7 Rxa2 3 Rh6+ Ke5 4 Rxc6** Two pawns up! **4...Ke4** Black's king becomes more and more active, but... **5 Rxc5** (see diagram). Three pawns up.

Black is three pawns down, but both his king and his rook are active. How does he make a draw?

Exercise 2: The next ending that made a big impression on me in terms of the power of an active king was in one of my games: I was Black against Tony Miles at Ostend 1991. Get that king active!

Exercise 3: McDonald-Sadler, Lloyds Bank Masters, London 1993. Black's pawns are impressive, but how can he get them to move forward? Find Black's next move!

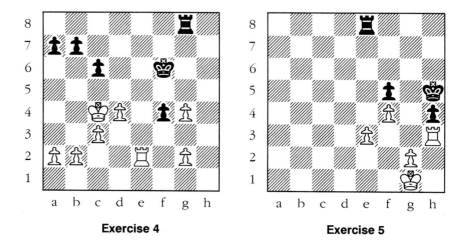

Exercise 4   Exercise 5

Exercise 4: Sadler-Turner, British Championship, Hove 1997. White is material up, and clearly should win, but which is the best way?

And finally, a nice trap, and a word of warning: you do have to be careful with your active king sometimes!

Exercise 5: Sadler-Onischuk, Cuxhaven 1994. White played **1 g3** Is it safe for Black to take on e3?

Summary

When you transpose from the middlegame to the endgame, take a few minutes out just to try to get yourself into a calm frame of mind.

If you are a pawn up in the ending, you should be enjoying the position a lot more than your opponent. Being material up should be *fun!* Having a good position should be *fun!*

You always want to create passed pawns far away from the opponent's king.

We have said throughout the book how crucial it is to try to bring all your pieces into the action, and this is especially true in endings – you have so little firepower, you can't afford to waste any!

Chapter Ten

Training and Thoughts for the Future

- Training 'Instant Vision'
- Lessons from Your Games
- Using Chess Books

My aim throughout this book has been to give you a feel for the game of chess: an understanding of the general shape of the game, the aims within each phase of the game. Essentially, this is the sum of my experience: it is how I see chess now after many years of work, using trial and error! However, I still have to answer the question that is most frequently put to me at chess tournaments: 'I want to improve, but I don't know how to work at chess. Tell me how!' Well, this is how I do it... I hope it helps!

Training 'Instant Vision'

Although I am a strong player, I have never made it to the very top of the game. But... I knew all the people who did! Although each of the top players had their own particular qualities, the gift I most wanted to steal(!) from players like Anand, Kramnik and Shirov was the speed of their 'instant vision' of the board.

When you see a position for the first time, your survival depends on appreciating two elements in the position. These are

1. The relationships in the position
2. The little tactics on offer

Whenever I was present when Anand or Kramnik were analysing their games, the routine was always the same. We would reach a position on the board, and after a couple of seconds, they would start throwing the pieces around while I was still adjusting to the position! At some stage later on I would say something like 'Oh, but can't White do this move from the starting position?' and they would just tap on one of the pieces impatiently, to indicate that this piece could not be captured because of a tactical idea I had not grasped. It wasn't my fault: they were just going too fast!

Part of it is down to great natural talent, but a lot of it can be trained if you get into the right habits from the start. For me, I only realised this once I got into the top 20 and started to play against these players, so it is more difficult to change the way I think, but for you... everything is possible! In my view, this is the most important of all the skills. If you can see what can be taken and what the little threats are in the position with 100% accuracy and at the speed of light, then

1. You cut down your chances of blundering and making stupid errors, and

2. You leave a lot more time for the difficult things, such as trying to see deeper into the position. If you have to spend 10 minutes on each move before you can be sure that you are not missing anything, not only do you start to play painfully slowly, but... it affects your confidence as well.

How do you train this? I have developed a few simple exercises that seem to increase my sharpness for the game.

The basic principle is that you should not be happy with just completing a task. Once you can do it, try to do it faster, better, make it look and feel easier. That is just what Kramnik and the other stars are doing compared to me... and it hasn't worked out badly for them!

Exercise 1: Training for relationships in the position

This is a beautifully simple exercise. I take a chess book with diagrams in it, and I go through each diagram in turn. At each diagram, I set myself the following tasks:

1. To show which of my pieces are attacking the opponent's, and vice versa.

2. To show which pieces are defending other pieces for both sides.

In other words, to appreciate all the connections that exist between the pieces in the position.

After a few diagrams, once it starts to feel natural, try to be faster, to pause less, to be more confident. And then, after you have done quite a few, if it becomes too easy or too dull, then add another element:

3. Show the squares that pieces are attacking or defending as well.

Let's see it in practice!

We can start by considering the position in diagram 1, which arises from a very sharp line in the Parma variation of the Nimzo-Indian Defence. Let us look and see how the relationships between the pieces are working:

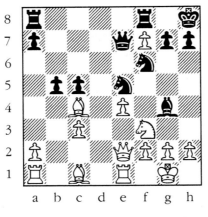

Diagram 1
A sharp opening variation

1: White Attacks
The bishop on c4 is attacking the black pawn on b5.
The knight on f3 is attacking the knight on e5.

1: Black Attacks
The pawn on b5 is attacking the bishop on c4.
The knight on e5 is attacking the bishop on c4, the knight on f3 and the pawn on f7.
The bishop on g4 is attacking the knight on f3.
The queen on e7 is attacking the pawn on f7.
The rook on f8 is attacking the pawn on f7.
The knight on f6 is attacking the pawn on e4.

2. White Defences
The queen on e2 is defending the knight on f3, the bishop on c4, the rook on e1 and the pawns on a2, e4 and f2.
The rook on e1 is defending the queen on e2 and bishop on c1.
The bishop on c4 is defending the queen on e2 and the pawns on f7 and a2.
The knight on f3 is defending the pawn on h2.
The rook on a1 is defending the pawn on a2 and the bishop on c1.
The king is defending the pawns on g2, f2 and h2.

2. Black Defences
The king on h8 is defending the pawns on g7 and h7.
The queen on e7 is defending the rook on f8, the knights on e5 and f6 and the pawns on c5 and a7.

The knight on f6 is defending the pawn on h7 and the bishop on g4.

The knight on e5 is defending the bishop on g4.

The rook on a8 is defending the pawn on a7 and the rook on f8.

The rook on f8 is defending the rook on a8.

3. White – Squares Attacked

The queen on e2 is covering a2, b2, c2, d2, f2, f1, f3, d1, d3, c4, e1, e3 and e4.

The rook on e1 is covering c1, d1, f1 and e2.

The rook on a1 is covering a2, b1 and c1.

The bishop on c1 is covering b2, a3, d2, e3, f4, g5 and h6.

The bishop on c4 is covering a2, b5, b3, d5, e6, f7, d3 and e2.

The knight on f3 is covering e1, d2, d4, e5, g5, h4 and h2.

The king on g1 is covering f1, h1, f2, g2 and h2

3. Black – Squares Attacked

The king on h8 is covering h7 and g7.

The queen on e7 is covering f7, f8, f6, e8, e6, e5, d6, d8, d7, c7, b7, a7 and c5.

The rook on a8 is covering a7, b8, c8, d8, e8 and f8.

The rook on f8 is covering g8, f7, e8, d8, c8, b8 and a8.

The knight on f6 is covering e4, d5, d7, e8, g8, h7, h5 and g4

The knight on e5 is covering c4, c6, d7, f7, g6, g4, f3 and d3.

The bishop on g4 is covering f3, h5, h3, f5, e6, d7 and c8.

NB. We do not need to consider that the black king covers g8 since to move there would be an illegal move. Likewise, the white rook on e1 does not cover the king on g1, because if the king is attacked by check, the fact that it is defended counts for nothing.

This exercise can be done anywhere – on the train, or outside in the sun. And it really is useful in so many different ways. You see an awful lot of chess positions (you get through a lot of diagrams with this exercise!) which is always useful. Moreover, you find that at the board you tend to see a lot more ideas and possibilities, simply because so many ideas come from the simple fact of something being attacked. Just 10 or 15 minutes a day is very useful. If you want to do more, then... it helps even more!

Exercise 2: Training for little tactics

When you are trying to work out what to do in a position, small tactics are a little like mosquitoes. They don't look too threatening, but they can be so irritating! Every player, weak and strong, has a few bad memories about spending half an hour in a difficult position, calculating complicated lines... before discovering that a simple move at the start for the opponent ruins everything! What sort of thing do I mean? Well, take this example from one of my recent games.

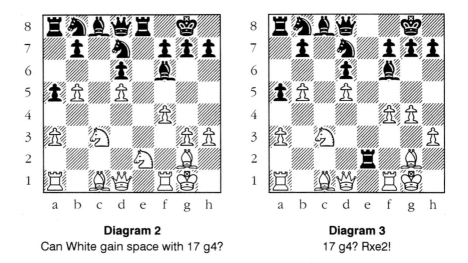

Diagram 2
Can White gain space with 17 g4?

Diagram 3
17 g4? Rxe2!

This is the position from Sadler-Topalov, Tilburg 1998. I was very happy with my position, and I wanted to carry on gaining kingside space. So I wanted to play

17 g4 (see diagram 2)

I spent some time thinking about the various defences that Black could adopt. Fifteen minutes in, something screamed to me in my head: '*You idiot!*' What was I missing?

17 g4 Rxe2! (see diagram 3) **18 Qxe2** 18 Nxc3 Bxa1 wins the rook in the corner! **18...Bxc3 w**ins two pieces for the rook which is favourable for Black.

So I played the consolidating 17 Ra2 first, getting out of the line of the bishop on f6, and then played 18 g4 on the *next* move... but it was very close!

So how do you train yourself to avoid this type of thing? For this, it is useful to have a book of tactical exercises. I have always used *Test Your Chess IQ* by August Livshitz (published by Everyman Chess in three volumes), but there are many others. I will demonstrate using a practical example (see diagram 4).

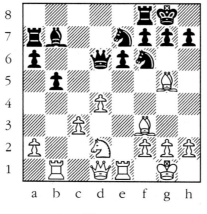

Diagram 4
Can you find White's tactical win?

This is the basic routine for the training:

1. Try to solve the problem yourself. Don't give up if you can't find it quickly!

2. If you can't solve it, look up the answer.

3. With the answer in front of you, try to work out how you *should have* approached the problem:

a) Discover what feature of the position should have alerted you first of all to the possibility of a tactic.

b) Break the tactic down into its component parts, so that you can see clearly what ideas were involved in making it work. Take notes of all these things and keep them in a chess folder, for example!

 Train your mind to approach positions in a consistently methodical manner rather than just trusting to luck that you will spot the crucial points when they arise!

In this example it is White to play. Make his advantage clear!

1 Bxf6 gxf6 2 Bxb7 Rxb7 3 Qf3! (see diagram 5)

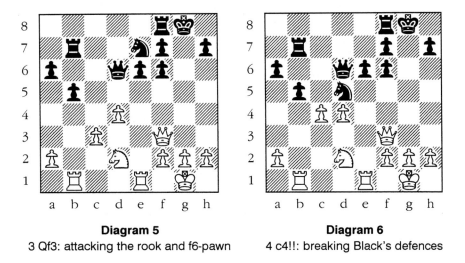

Diagram 5

3 Qf3: attacking the rook and f6-pawn

Diagram 6

4 c4!!: breaking Black's defences

Forking the rook on b7 and the pawn on f6.

3...Nd5 Both defending the pawn on f6 and blocking the attack of the queen on f3 on the rook on b7. **4 c4!!** (see diagram 6) Winning! Black's problem is as follows:

1. The knight on d5 is attacked by the pawn on c4. Something has to be done about this threat.

2. The knight on d5 cannot move. From d5, it not only defends the f6-pawn, but it also stops the queen on f3 from taking the rook on b7.

3. Black cannot capture the pawn on c4 because his pawn on b5 is pinned by the rook on b1 to the rook on b7.

Black is in dire straits. His best is **4...Qf4** but after **5 cxd5 Qxd2 6 Qxf6** Black's position is clearly falling apart.

What were the factors that alerted us to the presence of a combination, before we even understood the specific way of going about it?

1. The possibility of **1 Bxf6** forcing **1...gxf6** weakening the black kingside. Whenever you see a possibility like this, sit up and take notice! If the black king can be exposed, there is always a chance of something happening.

2. This should really get you excited! How can White attack the new weakness he has created? Well, it will have to be with either the *knight* or the white *queen* as the rooks are too far

away. Find the squares from which these pieces can attack the f6-pawn.

The knight can attack the pawn from e4, and the queen does it from f3. At the moment, f3 is taken by the bishop and 2 Ne4 is met by 2...Bxe4. However, by an amazing stroke of luck, with the simple capture **2 Bxb7** White gains a huge number of attacking benefits:

a. It removes the possibility of ...Bxe4.

b. It frees f3 for his queen.

c. It brings Black's rook to a square where it is attacked by the queen from f3.

These general positional considerations should set alarm bells ringing in our heads! Now let's take a look at the tactical motifs that arose in this passage of play.

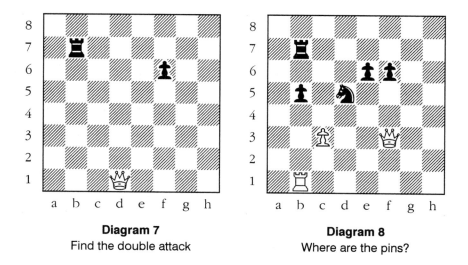

Diagram 7
Find the double attack

Diagram 8
Where are the pins?

Diagram 7: Find the double attack on the rook and pawn.

1 Qf3

Diagram 8: Name the pins in the position and find the key move that exploits them all.

The white queen pins the knight on d5 to the rook on b7, and the rook on b1 pins the pawn on b5 to the rook on b7. Therefore

1 c4!

This type of training will eventually pay off when you come to calculate variations.

 Complex calculation is simply a huge amount of these component parts put together. You need to be able to feel comfortable handling the essential small parts before you can be proficient at the more complicated things.

Lessons from Your Own Games

The games you play are your personal treasure-trove. It is through these games that you will learn the positions that you like to play, from the traps that you fall into that you learn best not to fall into them again! But people tend to make so little of their own games. After every game, they just file the score-sheet away and forget about it. Think of all the thoughts you had during the game, the worries that you had, the good ideas that you saw. If you make no record of them, they gradually fade, and you lose a great part of the things that you have created. The best players spend many hours, or even days and weeks, analysing the games they play and looking for improvements. This is obviously not possible for everyone, so for those without the time at their disposal for study that professional players have, I recommend the following routine.

Exercise 3: Making the most of your games

After every game you play, take five or 10 minutes just to think quietly about the game. Think about the flow of the game, places where you were afraid or uncomfortable, or the periods where your opponent played a good move or where you were proud of your play. The moments that spring to mind are the crucial moments in the game. Note them down in your chess folder. Draw little diagrams showing the position before each critical position. Underneath, write down the move that was played and a little description of why this is an important position. A few months later, you will come back to these positions in your folder and memories about the game will come flooding back!

For example, from my game against Topalov, I have the following 'snapshots':

Snapshot 1 (after Black's 13th move)

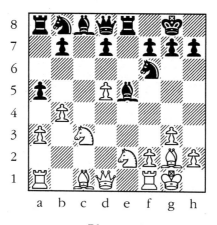

Diagram 9
How should White meet Black's ...a7-a5?

14 b5

A good move I think. It felt unnatural to occupy b5 with a pawn because it looks like such a good square for the knight on c3. However, by keeping the queenside closed, I make Black's queenside development much more difficult.

Snapshot 2 (after Black's 16th move)

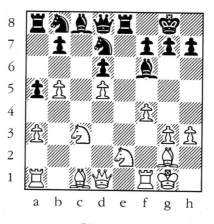

Diagram 10
How can White execute a kingside advance?

Ouch! I nearly played 17 g4 allowing 17...Rxe2!

Snapshot 3 (after Black's 20th move)

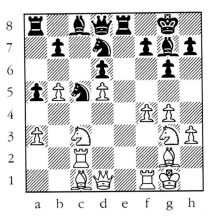

Diagram 11
How can White get the initiative?

Here I became rather indecisive, starting with

21 Kh2?!

Topalov pointed out to me after the game that 21 f5 followed by Ne4 would have given White a powerful initiative.

Undoubtedly, you will discover a few mistakes and fresh ideas just by looking over your own games. It really works for me!

The final stage is:

Using Chess Books

Reading chess books is not to everyone's taste, but it was something that really helped me to improve when I was nine or 10. When I say *read* chess books, that is precisely what I mean! I didn't play through all the games, take notes and try to absorb lessons. That is no fun when you're young! I just enjoyed reading books about the old players, finding out about their lives, seeing diagrams of their famous combinations. Or I liked self-assessment books (such as *Test Your Chess IQ*) where you had to find the correct answer.

Reading like this helped my general chess 'culture'. By doing this, you see a lot of positions, and it sparks something in your mind, fires your imagination... well, it did for me! So this is my list of favourite books: the books that were special to me in the development of my chess career. I hope they help you as well!

An Opening Repertoire for White by Raymond Keene and David Levy (Batsford)

This excellent book formed the basis of my white opening repertoire when I was 12 or 13 and provided a very good introduction to main line 1 d4 and 2 c4 openings. Highly recommended.

Endgame Strategy by Mikhail Shereshevsky (Everyman)

A lovely book! Simple, clear explanations of typical endgame strategies such as the queenside pawn majority, 'Don't hurry!' etc.

Chess Secrets I learned from the Masters by Edward Lasker (Dover)

Not the World Champion Emanuel Lasker, but his namesake, Edward. Entertaining stories about the great players of the 1900-1940 period with some fun chess thrown in. I loved this book!

Test Your Chess IQ (three volumes) by August Livshitz (Everyman)
Test your Endgame Ability by Jon Speelman and August Livshitz (Batsford)

Loads of positions with which to test and train your tactics and endgame skills!

Second Piatagorsky Cup by Isaac Kashdan (Dover)

At first sight, just a random strong tournament from the 1960s... but what makes it so interesting is that the players themselves all contributed notes to their games. There are many interesting insights into their thought processes during the game.

Zurich 1953 by David Bronstein (Dover)

Good notes without many variations and some great games! A really nice book.

Chess for Tigers by Simon Webb (Everyman)

Brilliant! I learnt my first insights into the art of practical play from this book. Entertainingly written with many useful hints.

My System by Aron Nimzowitsch (Dover)

A classic. To be honest, a lot of it is rather quirky, but the sections on pawn structure in particular made a deep impression on me. Not to be confused with *The System* by Hans Berliner which is not on my recommended list!

600 Chess Endings by Portisch/Sarkozy (Pergamon)

This was the endgame reference book I found easiest to get into. Clearly written with a good selection of endings.

All that remains for me is to wish you every success with your future chess adventures. Remember, you will make mistakes – everyone does – but make sure that you have a lot of fun at the same time. Good luck!

Chapter Eleven

Solutions to Exercises

Chapter One: Solutions

Exercise 1

Moves 1 and 2: 1 e4 and 2 d4. The white pawns occupy the centre.

Moves 3 and 4: 3 Nf3 and 4 Bd3 (or Be2 or Bc4 or Bb5). White develops his kingside pieces to good squares and this allows

Move 5: 5 0-0 getting the king to safety!

Exercise 2

a) 8 h4 has absolutely no point! It weakens White's king position by moving a pawn from the safety of the second rank to the exposed fourth rank. Moreover, it performs no useful attacking or central function.

b) 8 a4 does not put any pressure on the centre, but it does connect with Black's position, attacking the exposed pawn on b5. White's threat is 9 axb5 when 9...axb5 loses a rook to 10 Rxa8.

Exercise 3

This is a position from one of the sharpest openings in modern chess: the 'Rb1' variation of the Grünfeld Defence. Black has won a pawn, but in return White is ahead in development. I have chosen this example to illustrate how even in the sharpest positions, general principles still hold sway. White's best move is **13 Bg5!**

The pawn on e7 is the only unprotected unit in Black's position. So attack it, force Black to find a way to deal with the threat! For example, if Black plays 13...Nc6 to defend the e7-pawn, then 14 d5! chases the knight away, and after 14...Na5 15 Bxe7 White wins his pawn back!

13 Bg5 is a better way of carrying this out White's idea than 13 Bb4 as that move is met by 13...Nc6! when 14 d5 Nxb4! destroys White's pressure on the position. Always try to place your attacking pieces on squares where they cannot be threatened by your opponent's pieces.

Exercise 4

This is a position from my favourite opening: the Queen's Gambit Accepted. With 8 a4! White attacks his opponent's advanced b-pawn and forces Black to react. For example, if 8...b4 then White gains an excellent square on c4 for his knight, from which it cannot be driven away, with 9 Nbd2 Bb7 10 Nc4.

Chapter Two: Solutions

Exercise 2

This position is one of my own games: I was Black against Dizdar in the European Team Championship in 1997 and I was very happy with my position here. I have several *long-term advantages*:

1. White has isolated pawns on a4 and c5.
2. White has doubled pawns on e4 and e3.

Black also has isolated pawns on a6 and c7, but because they are very close to Black's position, they are a lot less vulnerable than White's weak pawns.

And my *short-term advantages...*

1. My rook occupies the open b-file. There are so many great squares for this rook on this file! From b4, for example, the rook would attack both the e4- and a4-pawns. Or from b2, the rook would cut off the white king on the first rank which could give Black some checkmating possibilities. Contrast this to White's rook on c1 which is tied to the defence of the sickly white pawn on c5.

The game finished:

29 Qd4 Qg5 30 Rf1 Attacking the loose pawn on f7. **30...e5! 31 Qc3 f6!** With these two moves, Black has fixed White's weak pawn on e4 – it can't move so it can't run away! – and neutralised any hopes may have had of developing pressure on the f-file by putting the f-pawn on a protected square. **32 Kg2 Qg4 33 Qc4 a5!** This avoids the attack of the white queen and secures the valuable b4-square for the black rook. **34 h3 Qd7 35 Qc2 Qc6** A perfect square for the queen. From here it attacks all of White's weaknesses: a4, c5 and e4. **36 Rd1 Rb4! 37 Rd8 Rxa4** and Black soon won.

Exercise 3

Black has a long-term structural edge because White has a doubled pawn on e5.

White has a substantial short-term piece advantage because he has pieces on the kingside and Black has very few defenders there. White is already threatening mate on h7 with 11 Qxh7 checkmate.

Chapter Three: Solutions

Exercise 1

There was checkmate!! Either after **2 Qxh7 checkmate** or again on move three after **3 Qxh7 checkmate**. The possibility disappeared when Black played 3...Nd3+.

Exercise 2

Black had **2...Nd2!** forking White's queen and rook! There was no need for him to defend the pawn on b7 – he could have just won material instead!

Exercise 3

Ooh, a lot of mistakes here!

a) First of all, after **3...Qf6** White had **4 Bg5!** winning the exchange! The queen on f6 must move **4...Qg6** and after the exchange of queens **5 Qxg6 hxg6** White captures the black rook with **6 Bxd8**.

b) Second, after **5 e4** Black could have played **5...Qxf4!** By playing 5 e4, White removed the protection of the pawn on e3 for the bishop on f4! This possibility was still open for Black on move six! He could still have played **6...Qxf4** instead of 6...Nb6.

Exercise 4

This one isn't easy, but it crops up *so* often! 1...Nb6 left the black bishop on c5 unprotected. This gave White the opportunity for **1 Bxh7+! Kxh7 2 Qc2+! Kg8 3 Qxc5** and White has picked up a pawn.

White did have an alternative possibility: **1 Qc2** forking the bishop on c5 and the pawn on h7. This possibility is less tempting in general because it is less *forcing*. The other line gave Black very few options: a check, another check, Black has to react, and before he knows it, White has won a pawn. Here, Black has just a little more time, and with time come extra possibilities... **1...Rc8! 2 Bxh7+ Kh8** What are Black's threats here? He has two:

a) 3...g6 trapping the white bishop on h7;

b) 3...Bxe3 discovering the attack of the rook on c8 on White's queen on c2.

Faced with these two threats, White's best is to play **3 Bd3 Bxe3 4 Qe2 Bxc1 5 Rxc1** when White still has a good position as, without the pawn on h7, Black's king is a little more exposed than it would like to be, but... he isn't a pawn up!

Well done if you spotted both possibilities.

Chapter Four: Solutions

Exercise 1

47 Qxd6! cxd6 48 b4! Three pawns against a rook is too much here, and the black king is too far away to help out! Now Black has several tries but nothing works:

a) 48...Kf8 49 b5 Ke8 50 b6 (threatening 51 b7 queening) 50...Kd8 (to meet 51 b7 with 51...Kc7) 51 a6! Kc8 52 a7 and the pawn queens; or

b) 48...Rc7 49 b5 Kf7 50 a6 Ke6 51 b6! Rxc6 52 a7 Rc8 53 b7 and the pawns get through.

In the game Black played **48...Ra7 49 b5 Kf7 50 b6! Rxa5 51 b7 Rb5 52 c7 Rxb7 53 c8(Q)** and White won in the end.

This was a very flashy way to win, and not strictly necessary, I guess – I did have an excellent position anyway. But it made a big impression on me – the way those pawns could defeat a whole rook by themselves!

Exercise 2

43 Bc6! would have won (as would 43 Bc8). The idea is that after **43...Bxc6 44 b7** (or 44 d7 Bxd7 45 b7) **44...Bxb7 45 d7** White has given up a bishop and a pawn, but Black cannot stop him from making a new queen.

Exercise 3

38 Rxc7! Rgxc7 39 Nxc7 Rxa5 40 b6 Ra2 41 Kc3 stopping Black from getting behind the pawn with 41...Rb2. The threat is now 42 b7. **41...Ra1 42 Nxd5** and Black resigned. For example, if 42...Kf7 (desperately trying to get the king towards Black's b-pawn) then 43 b7 Rb1 44 Nb4! blocks the rook! Black cannot prevent 45 b8(Q).

But what if Black had taken the knight with **38 Rxc7! Rgxc7 39 Nxc7** and now **39...Rxc7?** After **40 b6 Rb7** White's pawns are stopped as 41 a6 Rxb6 42 a7 Ra6 wins for Black!! In order for White to advance his a-pawn, his b-pawn must first be protected. The only piece for the job is the white king! So the plan is:

1. Bring the white king to b5.

2. Push the a-pawn... and win!

41 Kc3 Kf7 42 Kb4 Ke6 43 Kb5 Kd6 44 a6! Rg7 45 a7! White pushes the pawn farthest away from the black king. 45 b7 would have allowed 45...Kc7. **45...Rg8 46 b7** and a pawn will queen. The idea of sacrificing material to win with pawns against a rook is a very common ploy – as you can see, I've had it quite a few times! – so it is well worth remembering.

Exercise 4

In both cases, White has a huge structural advantage: Black has doubled pawns on a7 and a6, and isolated pawns on c7 and e6. Black's sole compensation lies with his extremely active rook on White's second rank which ties down the white rook to the passive defence of its queenside pawns.

The key point to appreciate is that if Black did not have his rook on that super-active post, he would stand terribly! Thus, with a bit of thinking we can see that, although Black stands well in the second diagram, he has a very nasty position in the first. Why? Well, let's play some moves from the first diagram:

1 Kf1 Ke7 2 Ke1 Where does the black rook go? It cannot remain on White's second rank and it has to retreat... **2...Rd5 3 Rd1** Here Black has no compensation for his weak pawns.

However, in the second example... **1 Kf1 Ke7 2 Ke1 Rc2!** Black's rook has just a little more space than before! When attacked by the king from e1, it can shuffle along the second rank. And if White gets annoyed and tries to push it away with **3 Kd1** then **3...Rxf2** wins a pawn. Since White cannot get rid of the black rook, he has quite serious problems as he can't do anything with either his rook or his king.

Chapter Six: Solutions

Exercise 1

With 2 c4, White puts pressure on the black centre and threatens 3 cxd5 Qxd5 4 Nc3 Qd8 5 e4 when he occupies the whole centre. By introducing such a threat and putting pressure on his opponent, White forces him to think and to react, and hopefully to make a small concession.

Exercise 2

With 3 g3, White prepares to develop his light-squared bishop on the long h1-a8 diagonal. This is not a bad move, but it doesn't put any pressure on Black's position. So this gives Black a little more freedom to develop his pieces. Here Black can play **3...Bf5** putting his light-squared bishop outside the pawn chain before developing his kingside with 4...e6 and 5...Be7.

Exercise 3

4...c5 is a typical move, to attack the white centre and **4...Bd6** is another! With the latter move Black attacks the bishop on f4 and forces White to make a decision: Does he capture on d6, does he move a knight to e5 or does he allow Black capture on f4?

I always like to play this way in the opening: to challenge the opponent right from the start to make decisions. Even if they are just small ones, your opponent can still get them wrong!

Exercise 4

With 9 dxe5, White:

1. Gains a tempo on the black knight on f6. By attacking a black piece and forcing it to move, White makes sure that his opponent cannot do anything positive with his move. Then on his next move, White has another chance to do something posi-

tive himself.

2. Chases away the king's knight from its defensive square on f6. This means that the pawn on h7 is no longer covered by the knight on f6 and the g4- and h5-squares are no longer covered by the knight, which allows the white queen to come to them, close to the black king.

Exercise 5

Whereas the bishop on d3 has a clear diagonal towards the black king, the dark-squared bishop on b2 is blocked by its own pawn on d4. If it wasn't there... **19 d5!** A very typical pawn sacrifice to open the diagonal for the bishop on b2. **19...Nxd5** The other captures are no better:

1. If 19...Qxd5 then 20 Bxf6 gxf6 21 Bh7+! wins the queen.

2. If 19...Bxd5 then 20 Nf5! Qf8 21 Nxh6+! (a typical attacking sequence – the pawn on g7 was connected to both the knight on f6 and the other pawn on h6, so by deflecting the pawn on g7 to h6...) 21...gxh6 22 Bxf6 (...you get to win your pawn back with a winning position). What is White's *biggest* threat? His main threat is 23 Bh7+ checkmate! Anyway, back to the game.

19...Nxd5 20 Bh7+! Kf8 21 Nh5! Attacking g7 in combination with the bishop on b2. **21...Ne5** After 21...f6 I was intending to sacrifice with 22 Nxg7! Kxg7 23 Qg6+! Kf8 24 Bxf6! with a huge attack – just look at those two bishops! **22 f4! Ng4 23 Bxg7+** with a tremendous attack. I won the game quite quickly afterwards.

Exercise 6

That's right! The super-solid **17...Nf8!** In the game, the knight also had an active part to play. After **18 N2f3 Qc7 19 a3 Rd8 20 b4** it came out with **20...Ng6** threatening to come into f4, and forced White to weaken his kingside slightly with **21 g3**.

Chapter Eight: Solutions

Exercise 1

Black's structural weak points are:

1. The central d5-square which Black cannot control with a pawn, and which White can thus seek to use for his pieces.

2. The backward d6-pawn which cannot be supported by any of its colleagues.

So how can Black try to 'repair' this weakness? How about **9...Be6**. Black's idea is to attain the structure after **10 Bxe6 fxe6** How successful has Black been? Very successful!

1. The new pawn on e6 covers the d5-square and prevents a white piece from coming there

2. By attacking the d5-square, the new pawn on e6 supports the advance of the d6-pawn from d6 to d5.

Exercise 2

Black's weakness is the pawn on b5. Though it is of course not such a clear weakness as the d5-square in the previous exercise, it has advanced further than Black would like, which means that it is slightly vulnerable to attack by a2-a4, for example, as we have seen earlier in this book.

As we saw in Chapter 2, pawns are at their best when they are standing side by side, ready to support each other when attacked. So Black's most common plan is to move his knight from c6 in order to move his c-pawn to c5. **9...Na5 10 Bc2 c5** This has three results:

1. Once White plays his pawn to d4, Black will have two forms of central pressure already: the pawn on c5 and the pawn on e5.

2. By putting two pawns on his fourth rank, side by side, Black gains queenside space and disguises the weakness of the b5-pawn — it seems part of a whole plan, rather than just sticking out like a sore thumb. In this way, Black makes a virtue of the loosening move ...b7-b5.

3. The knight manoeuvre chases the bishop on b3 from its excellent diagonal to a much less active square on c2.

Exercise 3

7 e5! is a very annoying move for Black. If Black does not take the pawn with **7...Nd7** then **8 e6!** is very uncomfortable for him, while after **7...dxe5 8 Nxe5** White is ready to recapture the pawn with Bxc4, and he has given Black a weak isolated pawn on c5 while bringing his knight to a commanding central square. The white pawn on d5 is isolated too, it is true, but it does provide the white knight with a superb outpost on c6 later.

Exercise 4

White has a rather tender spot on b3: White's a-pawn is no longer defending it, and the (extra) black pawn on c4 is attacking it... **4...Nc6! 5 d5 Na5!** The knight protects the c-pawn, and thus holds on to Black's extra pawn, and aims for the b3-square. This is not nice for White!

Exercise 5

White's pawn on d5 provides a rather tempting outpost on e6 for a white knight, so... **12 Ng5! 0-0 13 Ne6 Rfc8 14 f3** Supporting the central e4-pawn. The knight on e6 is extremely annoying for Black.

Exercise 6

Yes! **18...Nxf2! 19 Bxf2 Bxd3** wins a pawn! If **19 Bxf5** instead, then **19...Qxd1! 20 Rxd1 Nxd1 21 Rxd1 Nxf5** leaves Black a lot of material up!

Chapter Nine: Solutions

Exercise 1

5...f4! Black wants to get his king still closer to the white king via the f3-square. However, if 5...Kf3 immediately then 6 Rxf5+ is rather nasty! The extra pawn sacrifice means that after **6 exf4** (four pawns up!) then **6...Kf3** is possible without being disturbed by the white rook. The threat is 7...Ra1+ mate. How does White deal with it? White has only one way: he must move his h-pawn. **7 h3** and the game ended in a draw by repetition after **7...Ra1+** as after **8 Kh2 Ra2+ 9 Kg1 Ra1+** neither side is able to deviate. White was four pawns up, but Black's active king compensated for it. It just shows the power of an active king!

Exercise 2

40 Kd3 Ra2 And again! **41 Ke4! Rxh2** And again! **42 Kd5** The king is excellent here: it supports the passed e-pawn and attacks the isolated Black c-pawn. After this black pawn goes,

White will have a passed c-pawn as well. The game continued **42...Rg2 43 e4 Rxg3 44 e5 h5 45 Kd6** to shepherd the e-pawn home to queen. In the end, the problems proved too great for me and I lost the game. But it was a good lesson!

Exercise 3

Not **46...f3??** when **47 Rh4+!** is rather annoying as 47...Kxh4 is stalemate! Wherever Black's king goes, White can offer Black the chance to take his rook, e.g. 47...Kg5 48 Rh5+ Kg6 49 Rg5+. I didn't want to allow such a possibility, especially when I had such a thematic move to play! *Go for it!*

46...Kg3! Keeping White's pieces boxed in: I didn't want to let White play 46...Kf3 47 Rh3+. **47 Rh5 f6!** Taking away a couple of squares from the white rook. **48 Rf5 Kf3** Threatening ...e3-e2+ and Black soon won.

Exercise 4

34 Kc5! Rxg4 35 Kd6! Rh4 36 Kc7! and Black's pawns soon fell: the king was also excellently placed for shepherding home White's extra pawn on the queenside!

As we can see, whenever there are holes in the opponent's position, the active king is a formidable piece in the endgame.

Exercise 5

No! After **1...Rxe3 2 g4+!** both checks the active black king and opens an attack on the rook on e3 at the same time. Black must lose the rook!